EXODUS 1947

RUTH GRUBER

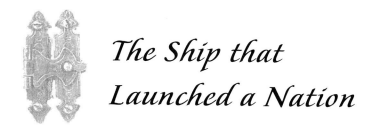

The Ship that
Launched a Nation

Formerly titled *Destination Palestine: The Story of the Haganah Ship Exodus 1947*

UNION SQUARE PRESS

An imprint of Sterling Publishing Co., Inc.

New York / London
www.sterlingpublishing.com

Dedication
For the people of the Exodus 1947
who made the voyage to Israel,
and for the Haganah men and women
and the American crew who took them there

STERLING and the distinctive Sterling logo are
registered trademarks of Sterling Publishing Co., Inc.

Library of Congress Cataloging-in-Publication Data Available

10   9   8   7   6   5   4   3   2

Published by Sterling Publishing Co., Inc.
387 Park Avenue South, New York, NY 10016
© 1948, 1999 by Ruth Gruber
Preface © 2007 by Blanche Wiesen Cook
Distributed in Canada by Sterling Publishing
c/o Canadian Manda Group, 165 Dufferin Street
Toronto, Ontario, Canada M6K 3H6
Distributed in the United Kingdom by GMC Distribution Services
Castle Place, 166 High Street, Lewes, East Sussex, England BN7 1XU
Distributed in Australia by Capricorn Link (Australia) Pty. Ltd.
P.O. Box 704, Windsor, NSW 2756, Australia

This work was originally published, in different form,
as *Destination Palestine* by Current Books, Inc., in 1948.
All photographs by Ruth Gruber.
All photographs and illustrations courtesy of the author.

Sterling ISBN-13: 978-1-4027-5228-5
        ISBN-10: 1-4027-5228-8

For information about custom editions, special sales, premium and
corporate purchases, please contact Sterling Special Sales
Department at 800-805-5489 or specialsales@sterlingpub.com.

Praise for Ruth Gruber's Youthful Accomplishments, Her Career as a Trailblazing Woman Journalist, and *Exodus 1947*

"When the gangplank went down on the steamship *St. Louis* an attractive Brooklyn girl of twenty years stepped ashore bearing a coveted degree of Doctor of Philosophy. . . . [Ruth Gruber] is now the youngest Doctor of Philosophy in the world." —*The New York Times*, August 15, 1932

"Ruth Gruber's return from the University of Cologne, Germany, with a Ph.D. *summa cum laude*, has aroused a great deal of admiring public attention; but one discovers no surprise at its being a young woman . . . who has performed this extraordinary feat."
—*New York Evening Post*, in an editorial entitled "Sex and Intellect," September 18, 1932

"A gifted and courageous woman who rushed into the vortex of history." —Gloria Goldreich, author of *Leah's Journey*

"After a three-hour battle in which 150 were wounded and three died . . . Gruber caught up with the ship at the dock. The British . . . were sending the DPs away on three closely guarded 'hospital ships,' which actually functioned as 'prison ships.' . . . After a three-week stay in scorching heat in southern France . . . the British sent them back to English prison camps in northern Germany . . . Back to hell. Gruber's photograph of the refugees' unfurled Union Jack with a swastika painted on it became *Life* magazine's Picture of the Week . . . Ironically, Gruber's original reporting, titled, "Destination Palestine: The Story of the Haganah Ship *Exodus 1947*," was written for the *New Yorker* and edited by William Shawn . . . One day, over lunch at the Algonquin Hotel, Shawn had some bad news for Gruber: Raoul Fleishman, the magazine's Jewish owner, had read her piece and rejected it [as] 'too Jewish.' Then Shawn [told her], 'I called my friend Bruce Bliven at *The New Republic* and . . . he said he would publish it.' To this day, none of Gruber's books that mention the British role in the creation of Israel [nor the *Life* magazine Picture of the Week] have been published in England."—Maureen Orth, *Vanity Fair*, February 2001

"Her personal odyssey is an inspiration."—Faye Sholiton, *Cleveland Jewish News*

"Has the word 'impossible' ever been in Ruth Gruber's vocabulary? . . . Gruber's reporting is vivid, a document of the self. . . . Empathy and tenacity are at the very core of her ability as a reporter; she does not hide her own outrage and passion. . . . Most famously, she . . . inspire[s] Leon Uris to write his novel [*Exodus*]."—Marie Brenner, from her introduction to *Ahead of Time* by Ruth Gruber

"Ruth Gruber's classic, *Exodus 1947*, is one of the most outstanding books to emerge from World War II, and should be in every Jewish [home and] library."—Leon Uris, author of *Exodus*

"This updated edition of Ruth Gruber's classic is most welcome. . . . One of the most compelling stories of modern history."—David Wyman, author of *The Abandonment of the Jews*

"It is one of the most moving books I have read this year . . . no other writer we know of has given [the story of the DPs] such compelling form and clarity."—*The New York Times*, September 28, 1948, reviewing the first edition of *Exodus 1947*, then titled *Destination Palestine*

Contents

LIST OF PHOTOGRAPHS

A Life of Vision and Courage

As issues of war and peace, justice and vengeance tear at our hearts, Ruth Gruber's *Exodus 1947: The Ship That Launched a Nation* offers the benefit of wise perspective and deep concern. Ruth Gruber has always been fiercely independent and powerfully talented. Born in 1911 in what she calls the "shtetl of Williamsburg, Brooklyn," she was an adventurous rebel who defied tradition, challenged authority and confronted danger. As this book goes to press, Gruber is still working at ninety-six—writing, speaking, and fighting for justice.

The first volume of her memoirs, *Ahead of Time: My Early Years as a Foreign Correspondent*, detailed Gruber's youthful triumphs and struggles. After graduating from high school at fifteen, then New York University at eighteen, she earned a master's degree in German literature from the University of Wisconsin. She then completed a pioneering dissertation on Virginia Woolf at the University of Cologne in Germany, at twenty becoming famous as the youngest PhD in the world.[1] It was 1932: She returned to the U.S. The Depression raged. Gruber could not get a teaching position.

Ruth Gruber became a journalist and never looked back. Leading newspapers competed for her stories, and she went where no foreign correspondent had gone before, including the Soviet Arctic and the gulags. She returned to Hitler's Germany and met Jews who were eager to leave but were blocked by harsh immigration barriers, including the bitter U.S. policy of delay and denial.

As a photojournalist, she was mentored by the best. Photographer Edward Steichen urged her to "take pictures with your heart." Every picture Gruber took, every word she wrote, was from the heart. The second volume of Gruber's memoirs, *Inside of Time: My Journey From Alaska to Israel*, opens with her 1941 assignment to Alaska for a *New York Herald Tribune* series. That assignment was transformed when Franklin D. Roosevelt's secretary of the interior

[1] Republished in 2005 as *Virginia Woolf: Her Will to Create as a Woman.*

Harold Ickes, impressed by her 1939 book *I Went to the Soviet Arctic*, hired her to do reports for the U.S. government instead.

Gruber's adventures in Alaska are fascinating. The Inuit and Aleut taught her how to live "inside of time" and record the realities of everything she witnessed. She protested tribal poverty and the humiliations of segregation in the military; she opposed environmental plunder, such as the seal killings on the Pribilof Islands, and challenged a contemptuous macho culture in Alaska. In this book, she detailed her efforts on behalf of refugees during and after the war.

In recent years, Gruber has become known to popular audiences as the woman played by Natasha Richardson in the CBS miniseries *Haven*, based on her 1983 book of the same name. In 1944, while "[Adolf] Eichmann was in Hungary selecting 550,000 Jews for death in Auschwitz," Gruber had an epiphany aboard the army troop transport *Henry Gibbins* sailing from Italy with nearly a thousand refugees who had come from eighteen countries Hitler had overrun. They were headed for a former army camp called Fort Ontario in Oswego, New York: "Standing alone on the blacked-out deck . . . I was trembling with the discovery that from this moment on my life would be forever bound with rescue and survival. I would use words and images, my typewriter and my cameras as my tools. I had to live the story to write it, and . . . if it was a story of injustice, I had to fight it."

After VE day, panic spread throughout the camp. Before boarding the *Henry Gibbins*, the refugees had signed a release to guarantee they would return to their countries of origin as soon as the war ended. Now the Justice Department, State Department, War Department, and Treasury Department all insisted that they must go back. But the countries they had left were no longer the countries they knew.

Secretary of the Treasury Henry Morgenthau, Jr., who had promised Roosevelt that the refugees would be returned to their homelands, told a group of humanitarian leaders Ruth had brought to his office, "I cannot sleep with my conscience if I go back on my promise to the dead president." Yet to ship refugees to certain deprivation and possible persecution seemed inhuman folly. After pressure from people like Ickes, Eleanor Roosevelt, and Gruber,

President Truman cancelled the edicts of the State and Justice departments, and the Oswego refugees were safe.

From 1946 to 1948, as chronicled in *Exodus 1947*, Gruber traveled throughout Europe and the Middle East first for the *New York Post* and then for the *New York Herald Tribune*, covering the Anglo-American Committee of Inquiry and the U.N. Special Committee on Palestine (UNSCOP). In 1946, President Truman asked Britain's prime minister, Ernest Bevin, to open Palestine to 100,000 displaced persons. Bevin agreed, provided the committee voted unanimously to open the gates. The vote was unanimous. But Bevin reneged and Truman became furious. Gruber's description of Truman's failed negotiations with Britain—the regional tensions, the stunning needs, the layers of suffering—do much to explain the ongoing agony of this divided, tormented land. Her photographs of the DPs are wrenching and disturbing. During this period, she became the foremost chronicler of Europe's displaced persons.

Unwanted by America and dispossessed in Europe, virtually all the survivors still in camps wanted to go to Palestine. But Britain kept the doors shut. Gruber was overwhelmed by the misery of the people she interviewed, and astonished by the brutality of British foreign policy. She attended the Nuremberg trials of Nazi officials, and feared "mass suicide" among the refugees. She was there as anti-Jewish hatred soared throughout Europe, with propaganda and rumors that America was "sending German Jews to govern Germany and Austria in a military government." In Vienna, Gruber, an assimilated secular American Jew, felt Jewish in an entirely new way: "I was riddled with guilt and haunted by the thought of what we might have done to have prevented some of the slaughter."

Gruber journeyed to Cairo, Baghdad, and to Jerusalem—where the British patrolled in tanks and nobody walked freely. Dr. Chaim Weizmann protested on behalf of the Jewish community: "It had become a prison, a walled-in city like the Warsaw ghetto." Gruber's sketches of David Ben-Gurion, Israel's most prophetic leader, "a passionate visionary," and Golda Meir, tough, hard-working, dedicated, are compelling.

In Palestine, Gruber met two of her cousins from Poland. On a kibbutz in the northern Emek region, she learned how everyone in her mother's shtetl in the Wolyn province had been murdered. Jews of all ages were beaten, stripped, and shot, then shoveled into the river. Gruber was more determined than ever to have an impact: "I wanted my words and pictures to shake my readers."

In an article entitled "Palestine Today Is Ireland of 1921," Gruber wrote of the region, "The fierce hatred of the British, the concentration camp atmosphere, the destruction of civil liberties, the growth of a people's army—the same social and political explosives which made Ireland the tinderbox of the last postwar period, make Palestine the time bomb of this one."

Ruth Gruber traveled with UNSCOP for four months during the most intense negotiations. Now there were differences among the Jews. Weizmann recommended a two-state solution: partition Palestine into a Jewish state and an Arab state. Others preferred one bi-national state, a secular democratic state of Jews and Arabs. At the time, Gruber wrote an article: "Divide the Land, and Let the People Grow."

Gruber received an urgent cable: the British had intercepted a refugee ship. She left the UNSCOP meeting in Jerusalem and drove up the crowded coastal road to Haifa. She saw the *Exodus 1947* limping into harbor and began taking pictures. The 4500 passengers were forced off the shattered vessel and placed by the British on "hospital" ships; Gruber knew better and wrote they were "prison" ships. She described the outrages: The ship had been rammed and boarded in international waters by the British Navy. One hundred and fifty were wounded. A sixteen-year-old orphan who threw an orange at a British soldier was shot in the face.

Then came waiting, and humiliations through a long summer. Her brilliant photographs and dramatic book, then called *Destination Palestine: The Story of the Haganah Ship Exodus 1947*, caused an intense stir. It was "the ship that launched a nation."

On May 14, 1948, Ben-Gurion announced the "world's newest Declaration of Independence," proclaiming the sovereignty of Israel.

Against both State Department and military advice, Truman recognized the new state. Ben-Gurion envisioned "terrible bloodshed," and, within hours, an Egyptian bomb fell on Tel Aviv.

Herald Tribune publisher Helen Rogers Reid sent Gruber back to cover the war, and the new migration. Gruber protested the creation of wretched tent camps often with no sanitation facilities. She interviewed women who cared for their babies in mud up to their knees. After meeting with Ben-Gurion, she sent him a report: "Jews are running camps for Jews, and they seem to have learned nothing from their own tragedy." The camps were soon replaced by decent housing, new towns.

Everywhere she went, Gruber bore witness, spoke bluntly, galvanized public opinion, and inspired people to action. Ruth Gruber's life story may help guide us through this tormented time when the brutal events in Israel and Palestine tear the heart out of her vision of peace and justice. And so the wars go on until hope and respect are restored; until it becomes possible to divide the land and let the people grow.

BLANCHE WIESEN COOK
New York City
18 May 2007

INTRODUCTION

Journalism—as in the time of Addison and of Swift—begins to take on stature, that of a medium which has both immediacy of impact and permanence of effect. By reporting what they have seen, with their hearts and minds as well as their eyes, journalism's gifted men and women sometimes give us literature-cum-journalism. Thus Ruth Gruber's vitally important book almost takes its place with John Hersey's *Hiroshima*. It is certainly a classic, because it is an immortal story of a crucial hour of our tragic years.

I first met Ruth Gruber in 1946. The Anglo-American Committee of Inquiry on Palestine was sitting in London, listening to much the same stuff we had heard in New York. Ruth was Foreign Correspondent of the *New York Post*, assigned to the tour of the commission by Ted Thackrey. It is not too much to say that the *New York Post* deserves major credit for breaking the story and thus paving the way for an understanding of the problem.

We visited the displaced-persons camps of Europe. Afterward both of us saw, for the first time, the land of Israel, and the miracles that its people have done. Miss Gruber's personality, her warmth, are such that in these places to which she came for the first time she was welcomed as a friend.

Miss Gruber has lived in the outposts of the world. She knows many people. She is loved by them. As correspondent for the *New York Herald Tribune*, she lived and worked in the Soviet Arctic. She traveled aboard the Russian freighter which opened the sea route to Murmansk. As special assistant to crusading, honest, and progressive Harold L. Ickes, Secretary of the Interior, she spent some two years in Alaska and was the first woman to travel down the new Alaska Highway at the end of the war. In 1944, she went as representative of the United States Government to Italy, war-torn and exhausted, to escort to America the one thousand refugees whom President Roosevelt had invited to Oswego, New York. She worked with these refugees for eighteen months. It was her understanding and strength that helped them to become citizens in America.

The commission benefited greatly, I think, from Miss Gruber's accumulation of experience. She arranged for members of Haganah, Irgun Zvai Leumi, and the Stern group to meet and talk with some of us informally.

She brought us also into contact with young Moslem intellectuals who were opposed, as violently as they dared to be, to the policies of the reactionary Arab leaders.

She struggled with British officialdom and almost succeeded in becoming the first non-Moslem woman to enter the sacred city of Mecca—and this would have been with the consent of the Government of Saudi Arabia. The ubiquitous Harold Beeley of the British Foreign Office intervened to bar her from Saudi Arabia after the Arabians had not only given her a visa, but also invited her to stay in the capital.

During all the months we traveled together through Germany, Austria, Palestine, and the Middle East, I learned to respect Ruth Gruber's integrity as a human being, her competence as a journalist. It was particularly fortunate, in my view, that she was assigned by the *New York Herald Tribune* to return to Europe and the Middle East in the summer of 1947 with the United Nations Special Committee on Palestine (UNSCOP). This was the hour when the opposing forces of Jewish desperation and British vindictiveness were to meet and clash in the deathless drama of the *Exodus 1947*.

The *Exodus* story, which Ruth Gruber tells in *Destination Palestine*, was a pivot on which world history turned. It was an act which revealed, fully and clearly, Bevin's anti-Jewish and pro-Arab policy. Simultaneously, it made plain that the Jews were a people, possessed of a new courage, an unshakable determination such as the world has rarely seen. In the fires of Auschwitz, fine steel had been forged.

When these years are written down, people will read and think of the *Exodus 1947* in the same terms as the Tea Party in Boston Harbor. It was, indeed, an hour of high courage. A people often wronged, frequently betrayed, determined that, whatever the cost, the oppressor's yoke was to be cast off. Thus it was that a new nation was born in those hours when Britain's "slave ships" lay in the broiling sun off Port-de-Bouc; thus it was that Mr. Bevin became an unwilling, but nevertheless active, accoucheur in the delivery of that nation.

No other event in 1947 was as important as the odyssey of the *Exodus*. It made possible, in fact, the United Nations vote for a democratic state in Palestine, a Jewish state in that land. Ruth Gruber's eyewitness dispatches in the *Herald Tribune* and her horrifying photographs in *Life* magazine and in newspapers around the globe helped arouse the conscience of men.

In a certain sense, the triumph of the *Exodus* means much to us in America. American dollars bought the excursion boat which made that journey of fate. Americans sailed the ship, shared her perils. One of them, Bill Bernstein of San Francisco, gave his life for the cause of the Jews, not because he was a Jew but because he believed in freedom for all people. There have always been Americans who recognize that freedom is indivisible. Liberty, as they know, must be helped wherever and whenever the good fight is possible. All of us today should walk a little straighter and prouder because of the people of the *Exodus*.

Israel is a reality. Israel and the world are fortunate that Ruth Gruber was there when that historic ship limped into Haifa Harbor. Miss Gruber has recorded its agony and its triumph in moving prose.

BARTLEY C. CRUM
Member, Anglo-American
Committee of Inquiry on Palestine
1948

EXODUS 1947

1

The DP Camps of Europe

 WORLD WAR II WAS ENDING. The armies of liberation stormed Auschwitz and other death camps. Some of the soldiers vomited, others fainted, at the sight of the walking skeletons and the corpses piled up like stacks of wood.

In the world outside the camps, there were many who assumed that the survivors would rush out of the gates, breathe free air, and live happily ever after. Nothing was further from the truth.

Those who could stand on their feet, and those who were healed, tried to return to their own homes. But the ghosts of their lost families hung over the streets. When they knocked on the doors of their homes, neighbors or strangers stared at them: "What? Are you still alive? Why didn't they turn *you* into a bar of soap?" In Kielce, Poland, forty-two Jews who had returned home were murdered in a 1946 pogrom.

The darkest chapter of history was still not over.

They knew they could no longer live in the towns and villages and shtetls where they had lived. So they went west—to Germany, the death land, because the Americans were there and the Americans would help them get to Palestine.*

---

* Since Palestine was the name used for the land now called Israel, I have continued to call it Palestine throughout this book.

They were DPs—displaced persons—a new category for stateless people on the run, housed in camps administered by UNRRA, the United Nations Relief and Rehabilitation Administration. They were aided by the American Jewish Joint Distribution Committee (or the JDC, known widely as the Joint) and guarded by the U.S. Army. Some of these DP camps were former Nazi army camps, horse stables, even death camps. DPs now huddled together, eighteen and twenty sharing one room with no privacy; four and five people sleeping on the very wooden shelves on which millions had died. The camps were a temporary refuge of desperation and hope.

From the end of the war in May 1945 until the birth of Israel in May 1948, nearly seventy thousand Holocaust survivors found their way out of the DP camps, crossing borders in the dead of night, trekking through forests and across the Alps until they reached secret ports in southern France and southern Italy. Here they climbed onto a motley fleet of obsolete warships, U.S. Coast Guard cutters, leaky fishing boats, cargo vessels, icebreakers, banana carriers, a presidential yacht named the *Mayflower*, and a small American steamer they named *Exodus 1947*—determined to reach the Promised Land they called Eretz Israel—the Land of Israel.

My life became entwined with refugees in 1944, when, as special assistant to Secretary of the Interior Harold L. Ickes, I was sent on a secret mission to war-torn Italy to bring to America one thousand refugees from eighteen countries Hitler had overrun.

"You're going to be made a general," Ickes told me. "A simulated general."

"Me? A general!"

"You'll be flying in a military plane. If you're shot down and the Nazis capture you as a civilian, they can kill you as a spy. But as a general, according to the Geneva Convention, you have to be given shelter and food and kept alive."

I flew to Europe in an air force plane, with real generals who were curious to know what I was doing on their plane. I told them I couldn't say. My mission was top secret.

In April 1944, Adolf Eichmann began deporting Jews from Hungary to Auschwitz. Now it was July, and he had already shipped 550,000 to their deaths, while we were bringing 1,000 refugees to life in Oswego, New York. We sailed aboard an army transport ship, the *Henry Gibbins*, also carrying wounded American soldiers. Hunted by Nazi planes and U-boats, we were in a convoy protected by twenty-nine ships, sixteen of them warships.

Day and night, pacing the deck aboard the *Henry Gibbins*, the refugees told me their stories of courage; of terror; of hiding in tunnels, in sewers, in forests; of risking their lives to save others. Often, tears wiped out the words in my notebook. The bonding with the refugees became the defining moment of my life. I knew from then on that my life would be inextricably bound with refugees, with rescue and survival.

Late in 1945, with the war finally over, President Harry S Truman learned of the abominable conditions in the DP camps. He asked Britain's foreign secretary, Ernest Bevin, to open the gates of Palestine to 100,000 DPs. Bevin, whose decimated country needed American aid, could not refuse the president. Instead, he suggested a new committee be formed, called the Anglo-American Committee of Inquiry on Palestine. It was the eighteenth committee to study the problems of Palestine. Made up of six Americans selected by Truman, and six Englishmen selected by Bevin, the committee had judges, lawyers, historians, and editors. Bevin promised Truman that Britain would accept their report—if it was unanimous.

Early in January the telephone rang in my office. It was Ted Thackrey, the editor in chief of the *New York Post* and husband of Dorothy Schiff, who owned the paper.

"Ruth, I would like you to accompany the committee as our foreign correspondent. Will you do it?"

My heart began to pound at the thought that maybe I could do something for the Holocaust survivors. "Ted, I'd love to do it but I have to check with Ickes."

"Call me back," he said, "as soon as you get an answer."

I called Ickes's appointments secretary. I told her it was urgent.

Here I am in a war correspondent's uniform on a four-month assignment in Europe and the Middle East to cover the Anglo-American Committee of Inquiry on Palestine, which had to decide whether Britain should open the doors of Palestine to 100,000 DPs.

She called back and said, "The secretary will see you immediately."

Ickes looked up as I walked across his vast blue rug, and he motioned me to sit at the right side of his desk. I learned later that he had no hearing in his left ear.

I told him of Ted Thackrey's offer.

"I heard about that committee," he said, "but I need you here."

"Mr. Secretary," I said, "as long as you need me, I will stay."

Thackrey was adamant. "You are the one to do this job. You know Washington. The American members of the committee will need all the help you can give them. You know the problems of the refugees. I'm not giving up."

On January 21, 1946, Ickes sent for me and placed a letter in my hand. I felt my face redden as I read Thackrey's letter explaining to Ickes why he should grant me a leave of absence. Ickes looked at me. "What do you want me to do?"

"You know, Mr. Secretary, as long as you need me, I will stay. But this is a chance to do something for the Jews who survived and are still suffering."

"Thackrey was right and I was wrong. You must go. You are the one to do this job. I will help you with Ruth Shipley over at the passport division and the War Department. Just leave your letter of resignation with me. When I resign, I will accept your resignation."

He extended his hand. "Good luck. I think the Oswego experience—helping those refugees cross the Atlantic, helping them overcome their fears and suspicions, and then helping them learn to live in America—was the best preparation you could have had."

With help from Ickes and Thackrey, my army orders and my credentials as a foreign correspondent came swiftly. I took the train to Brooklyn and broke the news to my parents.

Two years earlier, when I had been sent by Secretary Ickes to bring the 1,000 refugees to America, my mother had tried to prevent me from going.

On a Friday afternoon in July 1944 she had rushed down from Brooklyn to Washington. "My crazy daughter," she greeted me.

Left to right: Meyer Levin, the author; an unidentified woman; Gerold Frank of the Overseas News Agency; and Harry Beilin, the representative of the Jewish Agency, prepare to join others covering the hearings of the Anglo-American Committee of Inquiry on Palestine.

"Do I ever know where you are? Siberia? Alaska? Why do you have to go now?"

"Mom, I can't tell you. It's top secret. But maybe I can find your relatives in Poland and Russia."

It was not until the war was over that we learned, from one of my mother's relatives who had survived the massacre, that her aunts, uncles, and cousins had been driven from their homes in Poland. Led by a German officer on a white horse and beaten by German and Polish soldiers, the people of her shtetl, Beremlya in the Wolyń province, had been forced to march to the riverbank and strip naked. "Shoot!" the officer commanded, and shots splintered the air. Their bodies, riddled with bullets, were shoveled into the river.

Now, in January 1946, with peace in the world, my mother was as excited as I was that I was going to Europe. "Maybe," she said hopefully, "you can meet up with Irving in Germany. We're so proud of him." She loved telling how my brother, a captain in the army, had taken over a small hospital run by nuns in Bad Lipp-springe and turned it into a 200-bed army hospital for POWs.

The next day I went to the *New York Post*, where Thackrey embraced me. "I had to write that letter to Ickes," he said. "I knew we had to have you over there. You're going to be our eye-witness to what's happening to those survivors."

I flew in an air force plane to London, where I was told to get an army uniform immediately. At the army post exchange (PX), I changed into a khaki skirt, shirt, tie, Eisenhower jacket, raincoat,

U.S. Army officers entertain members of the committee in Germany. At my left is Dr. James G. McDonald, a refugee expert and later the first U.S. ambas-sador to Israel.

heavy army shoes, stockings, and an army brimmed cap with the insignia U.S. WAR CORRESPONDENT. The uniform was my ID. I needed no papers to enter the Royal Empire Society building, where the twelve members of the Anglo-American committee were sitting around a horseshoe-shaped table surrounded by journalists from most of the world. One of the journalists, Gerold Frank of the Overseas News Agency (ONA), and I were to be the only correspondents attached to the committee. Other journalists later joined us wherever we stopped.

I listened to the speeches as the Jewish leaders talked of the need for a Jewish state to house the DPs, while the Arab leaders talked of closing the doors of Palestine to all immigrants. With a tight deadline of 120 days to travel throughout Europe and write a

Bartley C. Crum, the San Francisco lawyer, becomes the best-known member of the committee when he predicts there will be mass suicides if the DPs are not allowed to enter Palestine.

report, the committee decided to split into four subcommittees: one to Berlin, another to the British zone of Germany, the third to the French zone, and the fourth to the American zone. My assignment was to follow Bartley C. Crum, the liberal Republican lawyer from San Francisco. He was joined by two Englishmen, Richard Crossman, the noted journalist, editor, and Labour member of Parliament, and Sir Frederick Leggett, a labor conciliator. They were to visit the DP camps in Germany, travel to Czechoslovakia, and then meet with the whole committee in Vienna.

Just before we were to leave London, Dick Crossman became ill and stayed behind for several weeks. Since there were no civilian planes flying, we had army orders giving us permission to fly in military planes. We flew to Paris and then on to Frankfurt,

Judge Simon H. Rifkind, U.S. district court judge and an adviser on Jewish affairs to General Dwight D. Eisenhower, is our liaison with the U.S. Army in Germany, Austria, and Czechoslovakia.

headquarters of the U.S. Army in Germany. I had time to get to know Bartley Crum, who was serious, courageous, and prepared like a trained prizefighter to battle for his convictions. He preferred drinking to eating, and was so good looking that people often turned to stare at him on the German streets. He was determined to find a way to solve the problem of the DPs. Sir Frederick Leggett, a slender man with British reserve, seemed equally eager to find a solution to the problems we were about to face.

In Frankfurt, we were joined by Judge Simon H. Rifkind, a U.S. district court judge, and an adviser on Jewish affairs to General Eisenhower. Frankfurt, the city of Goethe, music, and culture, was in ruins. I was shocked to see houses without roofs, rubble everywhere. Our planes had crumbled this once beautiful city. But when I saw women parading around in elegant fur coats, I wondered if they had been pulled off Jewish women's backs.

The army entertained us in high style. I telephoned my brother, Irving, who was with his unit in Stuttgart, and invited him to join me with a group of army officers for dinner. He held us spellbound as he told us how he had searched for Otto and Frieda Herz, the Jewish family I had lived with as an exchange student in Cologne. The Herzes' daughter, Luisa, living in New York, had asked me if he could find her parents. She gave him several possible addresses. One of them was in Bilthoven, in Holland. Irving knocked on an iron gate, aware that people were staring through a window. He kept calling out in his mixed German and Dutch, "I'm looking for the family Herz."

Finally a woman opened the gate. "Who are you?" she demanded.

"I am Ruth's brother. I'm looking for the Herzes."

She said breathlessly, "Wait a minute."

She called up the stairs, "Otto, Frieda, come down."

Two frightened, emaciated people walked slowly down the stairs, came through the gate, and fell upon him.

Irving tried to smile. "I am coming right back," he said.

He ran to his truck, drove into town, filled the truck with fresh fruits and vegetables, hurried back to the Herzes, and gave

As we enter the Zeilsheim DP camp, the refugees greet us with banners urging us to help them go home to Palestine.

Each DP camp we visit raises banners and placards. We learn that many of these DP camps are former concentration and slave labor camps. Now, brutally cold and slumlike, they seem filled with ghosts.

Men in the Neu Freimann DP camp outside Munich, wearing their concentration camp garb, show a mixture of frustration, anger, and determination in the banner they carry toward us: ENOUGH PRISON. *Behind them is a procession of DPs, two of whom are carrying a banner that reads* WE WANT PALESTINE AS OUR COUNTRY.

them food they had not seen for years. They told him about the man who had taken them out of Amsterdam and hidden them in the attic of a farmhouse. He was Johannes Post, a genuine hero who had saved their lives but lost his own. He was shot while trying to save a Jewish girl.

On February 8, 1946, our subcommittee entered our first DP camp, Zeilsheim, in the American zone ten miles from Frankfurt.

In army vehicles driven by U.S. soldiers, we were a small group: Bartley Crum, Sir Frederick Leggett, Judge Simon Rifkind, Major Ralph Strauss of the U.S. Army, Gerold Frank, and I.

In a driving rain, three thousand DPs stood before the administration building, calling out to us in accented English, "We want to go Palestine. We must go. We will go. It is our home."

With remarkable dignity and discipline, men, women, and children, some still wearing concentration-camp pajamas, paraded in front of us carrying banners: OPEN THE GATES OF PALESTINE. The people were living in slumlike, overcrowded barracks. Pasted on the front of the barracks were banners that bore such slogans as WE JEWISH CHILDREN WILL NO MORE STAY ON THIS BLOODY GROUND WHERE OUR PARENTS WERE KILLED. WE WILL GO HOME TO PALESTINE. We entered the office of Sylvan Nathan, the camp's UNRRA director and a former New York attorney, who told us solemnly, "In my opinion the entire camp wants to go to Palestine."

Outside again, children crowded around me, allowing me to take pictures. It seemed to me they had refugee eyes. They were orphans who had seen their parents murdered. They had seen the darkest side of life. Their eyes spoke of evil. A boy who looked about seven but who told me he was twelve, allowed me to hug him. I did not know who needed the hugging more, this beautiful boy who had no mother or father and who had no idea where his life would lead, or I, feeling his misery and loneliness. A woman came toward me and took my arm. "If rescue means life without a country or a future, then you should have let us burn in the crematoriums."

We visited the crowded living quarters, where four and five people slept together on wooden ledges stacked one atop the other. Crum walked beside me, looking angry. "The best thing to do is get rid of these DP camps as soon as possible. They are a disgrace."

The people waited patiently in the rain to say good-bye to us. They sang "Hatikvah"—their song of hope. We stood at attention as many of them wept. As our cars pulled away, someone shouted to us, "Don't waste time. Open the gates of Palestine."

Orphans in the Leipheim DP camp, a former SS stronghold between Stuttgart and Munich. The older orphans act as surrogate parents, protecting the younger ones. The eyes of the little refugee girl holding a toy tell of the evil she has seen. Can she ever regain her lost childhood?

More orphans greet us in the Kloster-Indersdorf DP camp. It is called a "children's camp"; they do not use the hated word "orphanage." Some welcome us; others stare, confused and suspicious.

Two children, one frightened, one impish. These children wait to be taken from the Zeilsheim DP camp, but no country wants them. Palestine is barred to them not by the British people but by British foreign policy.

In Stuttgart, a mother shows me her child's arm. "The Nazis," she says, "tattooed numbers even on our babies."

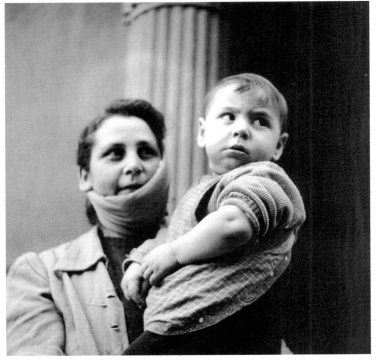

In nearly every DP camp in Germany, from Bergen-Belsen in the north to Dachau near Munich in the south, we saw a banner hanging on the wall with a poem written by Beryl Katzenelsen, one of the Jewish leaders in Palestine:

The bearded rabbi leads me through the DP camp at Bad Reichenhall while he speaks prophetically of going up to the Promised Land.

> With blood in our hearts
> We'll crush every wall.
> We'll allow no obstacles
> But we'll fulfill our hopes.

In the Landsberg DP camp, a woman in a torn but spotless housedress motioned to me to come away from the men in the committee. "You are a woman," she said. "You will understand the blood in our hearts. My husband went up in flames. I was rescued six times from the flames. I need a home. That is my hope. To go to Palestine."

I listened in silence.

She went on. "Maybe God has sent you and those men with you to help us crush the walls that block us"—she said the words like a prayer—"from going home to *Eretz Israel*—the Land of Israel."

In Bergen-Belsen, Dachau, Landsberg, Leipheim, Zeilsheim, Neu Freimann, and Stuttgart, the committee met first with the UNRRA officials and the representatives of the Joint. We learned of the problems, then toured the camps, sat with the DPs and listened carefully to their stories of how their families had been shot or burned or gassed, and then invariably asked the people, "Why do you want to go to Palestine? You know there is fighting. Arab riots. Why do you want to go there?"

A sixteen-year-old orphan in Bergen-Belsen gave us one of the most poignant answers. "Everybody has a home," he said. "The British have a home. The Americans. The Russians. The French. Only we don't have a home. Don't ask us. Ask the world."

The spirit that characterized almost every DP we talked to was a growing anxiety, an uncertainty of the future, a distrust of all humanity, and a resentment against the democratic world. "First they did nothing to save us," a man told us. "Now they do nothing to liberate us after liberation."

"That's just why we are here," Bartley said, then promised him, "We're going to find a way to get you out of here." The testimony that we were taking was becoming unbearably real. I made a silent prayer that we could fulfill his promise.

Landsberg, near Munich, the largest DP camp in Germany, held five thousand refugees, nearly all between the ages of twenty to thirty-five. They had been young and strong enough to survive as workers for the Nazis. There were almost no old people and fewer than a hundred children. The elderly and the children were always the first ones the Nazis selected for the gas chambers. Now the survivors improvised their own families—surrogate families where mother, father, and children might all be twenty-five years old. Later I learned that 120 of the young people we met in Landsberg were aboard the *Exodus 1947*.

A young woman with purple numbers on her left forearm approached me. "Why are you here? Have you come to stare at us as if we were monkeys in the cage? Or have you come to help us get to Palestine?"

"If you can't get to Palestine," I asked her, "where else would you go?"

"The crematoriums."

One night I slipped away from the committee to attend the first wedding of DPs at Bad Tölz, the headquarters of the U.S. Third Army, twenty-five miles from Munich.

Memories of gas chambers, death marches, and ghetto shootings filled the tiny hall as a violinist played Mendelssohn's "Wedding March," and the bride, dressed in a secondhand ivory satin gown, walked slowly toward the flower-decked canopy.

Chaplain Paul Gorin of Chicago, senior Jewish chaplain of the Third Army, performed the marriage ceremony. This little community of forty-seven Jews, whose lives were miraculously saved when American forces rescued them from a death march, listened with tears to the chaplain's moving sermon on the beginning of a new life and hope. Outside, snow fell on the pine trees and pastel cottages.

After the ceremony, the bridegroom, Judah Balaban, thirty-eight, from Pabianice, near Lodz, Poland, said to me, "You probably are wondering why I am getting married now. I have had the greatest tragedy a person can have. I was a husband and already had a family of three sons. All were burned in the crematorium at Treblinka concentration camp in May 1942.

"There were fifty in my family. I am the only member alive. My bride is the sister of my dear wife. In her eyes I see my wife's face. All over my room hang pictures of my wife and dead children. She doesn't disturb them because it is her family too.

"I am taking care of her as my wife would have wanted. She too is alone in the world."

The next morning I described the wedding to Bartley Crum. "These people," Bartley said thoughtfully, "will get there if they have to walk all the way. Many may die on the way, but sheer willpower will get most of them there. The movement has all the aspects of a children's crusade. I have never seen such fervor in my life."

A woman steps numbly over the cold shards of Munich.

A father leads his son past Munich's charred and gutted buildings.

Twilight in Munich. People push wheelbarrows toward the railroad station as they hurry past the bombed-out reminders of the war they started and lost.

In Munich, a city in ruins, Dr. Zalman Grinberg, president of the Central Committee of Liberated Jews, told us how he had hidden his baby son in a barrel in the ghetto of Kovno, Lithuania. The Nazis were rounding up all of the children and either stabbing or asphyxiating them. He smuggled the baby out to a non-Jewish friend. The war was still on in 1945 when the doctor was put on a train from the concentration camp in Dachau, headed for Auschwitz.

U.S. planes strafed the train. The Germans shot most of the people in the train, then fled. Dr. Grinberg, unhurt, rounded up the survivors and led them for a day and a half to a German village, where he demanded to meet the burgomaster. "I am the medical representative of the International Red Cross," he said. "I have people with me who need medicine, food, and shelter. I request you to turn over to me all necessary facilities at once."

When the burgomaster looked indifferent, Dr. Grinberg said, "The Americans are twenty-four hours behind me. If you don't give me what I demand, you will be hanging by the neck five minutes after they arrive." The burgomaster fled, and Dr. Grinberg took over the hospital.

He was one of the lucky ones. When the war ended, his baby was returned to him and he was reunited with his wife. But the scars from what he had survived were still raw. "Nobody who has not lived through the bestiality of concentration camps can even begin to understand what happened in them." I listened closely, watching his handsome but emaciated face as he threw his words at us, each one a spear.

"We had no hope of coming back alive, but in our weak hours we tried to imagine how it would be if some percentage of us should become free. We pictured how the world would stand up to help us, to comfort us, to console us, and to assist us in reaching our goal of Palestine."

We left Germany, shaken by his story.

We were in Prague interviewing U.S. Ambassador Laurence Steinhardt when he said, "You resigned from the Department of the Interior today."

I stared at him in amazement. "How do you know?"

"It came over the radio this morning. Ickes announced that he was resigning, and he accepted the letter of resignation you left with him."*

I was sorry to leave Ickes, who, of all the Cabinet members, had fought the hardest to open the doors of America to refugees

---

*It was later that I learned that Ickes had resigned following a bitter clash with President Truman over the nomination to a major post of an oilman who had attempted to bribe Ickes to obtain offshore drilling rights in California.

and, like everyone else, failed. But I was happy to be able to return to my first love, journalism.

From Prague, we set out for Vienna in a long convoy, but at the Czechoslovakian border, a guard halted us.

"Stop!" he shouted. "You're under arrest."

Judge Rifkind demanded to know the reason.

"We got a message from Prague to hold your convoy. They said you stole top secret papers from the government."

"Sheer madness—we just left the American ambassador in Prague. Telephone him and he'll clear everything up."

"Get out of your cars," the policeman ordered, "and we'll put you in the border guardhouse. We have only a field telephone and it takes quite a while to reach Prague by phone."

The guards were friendly, but their guns were fixed on us. In the freezing cold, they plied us with hot tea. We kept ourselves amused at the thought of being arrested while traveling with a district court judge. After several hours, the guard came in. "We got through finally," he said. "Yours is the wrong convoy. You're free to go."

Later the committee received an apology; it was explained that a U.S. military raiding party had stolen some documents that were needed for the Nuremberg trials.

We drove through snow-covered fields on the way to Vienna, reaching the city before any of the other subcommittees arrived. Bartley Crum suggested that Gerold Frank and I arrange a press conference for him. We gathered up all the foreign correspondents living in the press camp, and Bartley warned the press, "Unless the DP camps of Europe are cleaned out and the Jews are allowed to reestablish their lives, there will be mass suicides." The headlines shouted SUICIDE!

The next day Judge Joseph C. Hutcheson, the American chairman of the committee, and the British chairman, Sir John Singleton, Judge of the King's Bench in London, arrived in Vienna. Annoyed by the publicity Crum had received, they decided to hold their own press conference. "Everywhere we went," Judge Hutcheson said, "there was only one song: 'Zum Palestine, Nach Palestine.' Ninety to one hundred percent of the Jews want to go to Palestine." The son of a Confederate captain, raised in strict Presbyterian tradition, the judge spoke to me in rich phrases. "In me there is an absolutely stout feeling that justice is right and injustice is wrong." He continued, "St. Paul's dictum, 'Quench not the spirit, despise not prophesying, prove all things, hold fast that which is good,' is good enough for me or any man who calls himself liberal. I am exceedingly anxious that a just and final solution for the problem of the Jews in Europe and Palestine may be reached."

From Vienna we flew to Cairo and checked in at the famous Shepheard's Hotel. Palm trees waved outside my window. The sun flooded my room. After sleepless nights in Europe haunted by the images of the lonely orphans in the dark and ugly DP camps, I suddenly felt energy and light surge into my body. I didn't need sleep.

Swiftly, I climbed out of my army uniform, bathed in a huge bathtub, changed into a blue suit and a blue hat with a jaunty feather, and checked my oversize handbag to make sure there were enough notebooks, pens, and rolls of film to cover the day's sessions. With my Leica and Rolleiflex slung over my shoulder, I taxied to the elegant Mena House, where President Roosevelt, Winston Churchill, and Chiang Kai-shek had met during the war.

As the full committee assembled, guarded by police in red fezzes and soldiers with guns warning us to watch out for terrorists, we discovered that only Arabs were testifying. Bartley Crum decided to find out why. He soon learned that the chief rabbi and Catawi Pasha, one of the wealthiest men in Cairo, had been summoned to the palace by Egypt's monarch, King Farouk. They understood that it would be wiser not to testify.

The speeches boiled down to one argument: Palestine should be closed to the 100,000 DPs. These Jews who had survived the Holocaust were too Western. Egyptians were not pining to be westernized.

Evenings, the Arab leaders entertained us in their villas with musicians, belly dancers, and modern American jazz. Young Arab men in Western clothing asked me to dance, and on the dance floor they assured me Arabs were not anti-Semitic. "Indeed," they told me, "we are cousins. Semites together."

After the music, we were beckoned to banquet tables laden with Middle Eastern delicacies, including sheeps' heads. Not to embarrass our hosts, I picked at the food, and when I made sure no one saw me, I dropped most of it into my handbag. Despite my precautions, I still fell victim to Montezuma's revenge.

The hotel physician treated me with some shots that calmed my rampaging stomach. "You must stay in bed," he advised me.

"No time," I told him.

"You Americans." He shook his head. "I think you're all crazy. Anyway, don't be stupid. Just eat mashed potatoes and tea and toast."

I followed his advice, continued to attend the hearings, sending cables and photos to New York, and explored Cairo, a city of terraced homes and marble palaces for the elite, and mud huts for the poor, riddled with filth and stench and disease.

Late one afternoon, we boarded a slow-moving train leaving Cairo. I wished the train would speed up as I jotted last-minute notes on the hearings. After sixteen hours I squeezed my hands in anticipation. We were approaching the heart of the committee's work: the Holy Land.

The train stopped in Gaza where Samson, "eyeless in Gaza," had brought down the Philistines' temple.

Paul Mowrer, the *New York Post*'s local correspondent, met me with his car. It was spring, the air was sweet, and the people seemed full of hope as we drove up to Jerusalem. "The only way you can get to Jerusalem," Paul explained, "is by going up."

Going up.

I realized, as we drove up the narrow winding hills, that we were following the biblical going up from slavery to freedom, from Egypt to the Land of Israel. This was the *aliyah* that not only the DPs but Jews all over the world dreamed of when they prayed at the end of each Passover seder, "Next year in Jerusalem."

Jerusalem rose before us, a golden city of stone, yet a city under siege. The committee and several foreign correspondents who joined us settled into the King David Hotel, where we found ourselves surrounded by twenty-four-hour armed guards with submachine guns and CID (Criminal Investigation Department) agents. Soldiers manned the rooftops of the hotel and the luxurious YMCA across the street, where the meetings were to be held. Tanks carrying British soldiers patrolled the broad streets. Coils of barbed wire made whole areas impenetrable. The infamous "Black and Tan" police who killed Sinn Feiners in Ireland in the twenties had been recruited to police the Holy Land.

Palestine in 1946 is the Ireland of 1921, I cabled the paper: "This is a police state."

Most of the Jerusalemites who invited me to their homes made it clear they did not hate the British people. They admired them. They devoured British books and papers, studied Shakespeare, and, if they could afford it, sent their children to Oxford and Cambridge. It was the colonial policies of the British government that they hated. It was the soldiers they hated for breaking into their homes, searching for arms, and arresting people and locking them up in the formidable Teggart fortresses that cluttered the landscape. The mandatory government had already spent $20 million not on health and education and culture, but on jails.

The man they hated most was Britain's foreign secretary, Ernest Bevin. They did not know they shared that contempt for Bevin with President Truman.

In the twenties, when the Middle East was carved up between England and France, Britain had been given the mandate by the League of Nations to turn Palestine into a Jewish homeland. But in 1939, just as Hitler was sealing every escape route from Germany, Britain shut the doors of Palestine, the one country in the world whose people had their arms open for every fleeing Jew. Now Bevin was determined to stop "the invasion of Jews" into Palestine with tanks and guns.

As foreign correspondents, we too fell under the mandatory police tactics. We were told there was domestic censorship but none for us. Still, we were sure our stories were carefully scrutinized by British censors before they were wired to our papers.

Dr. Chaim Weiz-
mann, who will
become Israel's first
president (seated,
left), huddling with
David Horowitz, one
of his chief advisers.
Surrounded by
Jewish and Arab
leaders, he is
preparing to address
the Anglo-American
Committee of Inquiry
at the YMCA in
Jerusalem.

Each morning we had to apply to the Government Press Office for a new press card to allow us into the YMCA. We were told this was necessary. Should we lose our card and a terrorist find it, he could use it to enter the hall and kill us. We pretended to believe their excuse, knowing it was one more way of keeping tabs on us and learning what we were reporting.

The first witness was Dr. Chaim Weizmann, who would later become Israel's first president. Frail, nearly blind, but with a mind as nimble as a ballet dancer's feet, he spoke passionately.

"We warned you, gentlemen. We told you that the first flames that licked at the synagogues of Berlin would set fire, in time, to all the world."

He answered those on the committee who argued, "The Jews who survived should go back to their lands and rebuild them."

"European Jewry," he said, "cannot be expected to resettle on soil drenched with Jewish blood. Their only hope for survival lies in the creation of a Jewish state in Palestine."

I underlined his words as he linked the refugee ships to American history. "The leaky boats on which our refugees

The tension in the YMCA heats up as Weizmann (second from left) assesses the hearings that will determine whether Britain will open the doors of Palestine to 100,000 DPs.

come to Palestine are their *Mayflower*s, the *Mayflower*s of a whole generation."

David Ben-Gurion, the most prophetic leader I have known, spoke next. His voice, high and powerful, rang through the halls of the YMCA, and by radio entered people's homes.

"What do you mean by a Jewish state?" one of the committee asked him.

"By a Jewish state we mean Jewish independence. We mean Jewish safety and security. Complete independence as for any other free people."

Golda Meir, the American who would later become her country's prime minister, continued the case for a Jewish state. Her words, clear, logical, and forthright, described how Jewish labor and Jewish farming had changed the face of Palestine.

After the Jewish leaders, two Arab leaders spoke. One was Jaamal Husseini, nephew of the ex-mufti who had spent most of the war years in Germany with Hitler, helping to exterminate Jews. The other was Auni Abdul Hadi, former private

David Ben-Gurion, the head of the Jewish Agency, the shadow government the Jewish people have created for themselves under British mandatory rule, testifies before the Anglo-American Committee. He explains why the DPs are desperate for their own homeland where they can have security and freedom. He shakes his head vigorously when I tell him I think he is the Abraham Lincoln of his people. "No, no, not me," he exclaims. "When I think of a great man, I think of Abraham Lincoln. And who am I?"

secretary to King Faisal, who had signed an agreement with Dr. Weizmann declaring his sympathy for the Zionist cause.

Both men represented the self-designated Arab Higher Committee. Sir John Singleton questioned Husseini carefully. "Is it your wish that the British forces and police should be withdrawn from Palestine forthwith?"

When he nodded, Sir John went on. "Have you considered what would happen the day following? Quite clearly, bloodshed."

"I don't think so," Jaamal Husseini said. "If these pampered children, these spoiled children of the British government, the

Bedouin children traverse the desert near Amman. I ask them if they know this is a great day in their lives. King Abdullah, the grandfather of young Hussein who will succeed him soon, has changed the name of their land, Transjordan, to the Hashemite Kingdom of Jordan. The children do not understand a word.

Two Orthodox Jews walking in the narrow streets of Jerusalem's Old City, where Jews and Arabs live in their own sections.

Reba Horowitz, the wife of David Horowitz, the country's chief economist, escorts me through New Jerusalem.

Zionists, know for once that they are no more to be pampered and spoiled, then we will be friends, probably." A ripple of laughter went through the hall of the YMCA.

After long days visiting Jewish and Arab towns and settlements, the committee split up. Bartley Crum stayed in Palestine while others traveled to neighboring Arab states. I decided to go to Iraq and Saudi Arabia with Sir John Singleton, the British chairman of the committee, Major Reginald Manningham-Buller, Conservative Member of Parliament, and Frank Buxton, the Pulitzer Prize–winning editor of the *Boston Herald*. Buxton welcomed me. "It will be good to have you cover those hearings," he said. "The world must know how these two Arab countries, rich in oil, feel about immigration to Palestine."

"We'd have no problems in the Middle East," President Truman once told me as I interviewed him in his office in Independence, Missouri, "if not for that dirty three-letter word." He spelled it out slowly, "O-i-l."

How tragic, I thought, that the DPs, hundreds of miles away, waiting for the committee to decide their fate, were caught in the web of Britain's need for that dirty three-letter word.

In Baghdad, the hearings were held in secret in the Amanah municipal hall. The Iraqi government had selected the witnesses: a few Moslem clergymen, some politicians, two members of the Christian Communists, and two anti-Zionist Jews—Chief Rabbi Sassoon Khadouri and Ibrahim El Kabir, who worked in the Ministry of Finance and who invited me to his home to meet his wife.

She could have been serving tea in Paris or New York. Unlike the heavily robed Moslem women, she wore a fashionable dress that twirled around silk stockings and high heels. Laughingly, she said in flawless English, "People still think we live here like the people in the stories of the *Arabian Nights*."

Ibrahim El Kabir chose his words carefully. "Neither Rabbi Sassoon nor I speak for all the Jews in Iraq. We, of course, like the others, testified against allowing more Jews into Palestine—the position of our government. But nobody has the authority to speak for all the Jews of Iraq."

I understood.

Later I called on Chief Rabbi Sassoon, who looked like a potentate who had stepped out of a medieval scroll. He wore a tall silk turban and an elegant embroidered robe. With his physician son interpreting, the rabbi brushed my questions aside, blessed me for my work, presented me with a box of Arab sweets, and directed his son to show me around Baghdad. The interview was over.

While we walked along the crowded bazaarlike main street, Dr. Sassoon whispered, "Part of our family is already in Palestine. My father will stay, but the rest of us are making plans. We are not safe here anymore." He glanced over his shoulder and then, in a loud voice, pointed out the sights.

The next morning, I applied for a visa at the Saudi Arabian consulate. "We welcome you to our country," the consul spoke graciously, as he stamped the visa in my passport.

"Where will I stay in Riyadh?" I asked.

"Probably in the quarters of the women in the king's household."

"His harem?" That would be a new experience. There were certainly advantages to being a woman foreign correspondent, I thought. How much closer could I get to King Ibn Saud while I interviewed him about the relationship between oil and opening the doors of Palestine?

The consul smiled. "I suggest you obtain an *aba*." It was the long thin black wrap that covered Moslem women from head to toe. "And get a *yashmak*, a black face veil."

Frank Buxton was delighted. But Sir John Singleton was furious. In London, I had heard that Sir John had been known in Ireland as a "hanging judge." Often, listening to him question Jewish and Arab witnesses, I wondered how a hanging judge would treat the DPs in the final report.

"I am told," he said, "that the Saudi Arabians do not want women in their country."

"They invited me." I showed him my visa.

"I have no authority to take you."

"Who has the authority?" I wanted to know.

He walked away.

Harold Beeley, the British secretary of the committee and Bevin's chief Arabist, answered for him. "We are in charge. You cannot go."

Several years later, Frank Buxton wrote me that he regretted he had not fought harder to get me on the plane. It was a twenty-passenger plane with fifteen empty seats, and he had discovered that the United States was paying for it.

I returned to Jerusalem and rejoined the committee. They had finished traveling and were leaving for Switzerland to write their report.

In Lausanne, the twelve men spent a month in heated debate reliving what they had seen, often arguing bitterly, as they began the process of reaching decisions. From my sources in the committee, I was sure the Americans and Dick Crossman, the British writer and later an MP, would vote to let the DPs enter Palestine. But would the five other Englishmen do Bevin's bidding and bar the Jews?

On a sun-splattered morning in May 1946, the committee voted unanimously to open the gates of Palestine to 100,000 displaced persons.

In the DP camps, on the streets of Jerusalem, in the kibbutzim, people hugged and kissed and sang and danced, but joy turned bitter when Bevin rejected the report. On September 17, 1947, the British Colonial Office told the United Nations that Britain could no longer rule Palestine. The UN then created its own committee—the United Nations Special Committee on Palestine, known as UNSCOP. It consisted of eleven members, largely from countries that had no interest in Arab oil. For the first time, there would be no Englishmen involved in the decisions on Palestine's future.

The *New York Herald Tribune*, the paper I had reported for in the Soviet Arctic in 1935–36, before working for Ickes, asked me to return as their foreign correspondent and accompany this new committee. Again we traveled through the DP camps in Germany and Vienna, the Arab world and Palestine.

In Vienna, Dr. Enrique Fabregat, the delegate from Uruguay, asked me to accompany him as his interpreter to the Rothschild Hospital, which had been converted into a DP camp. One hundred Jews had descended on Vienna and were housed in the camp. "Most of us have come from Romania," a man in tattered clothing told me. "We're running away from anti-Semitism plus hunger. Famine creates anti-Semitism. They blame their hunger on the Jews."

A young man approached me. His eyes were bloodshot. He took deep breaths as if the words came up from his guts. "In Romania they killed some thirty thousand Jews in two hours. They took the Jews to the slaughterhouse. They hung them alive the way they hang cows, and they put knives to their throats." He drew his hand across his throat.

In Vienna, the Rothschild Hospital, overflowing with refugees, has been turned into a DP camp. One hundred Romanians have just arrived and are given new pails for lunch. A mother shields her daughter with her arm.

The mother is about to break down and weep. Her daughter leans close to comfort her.

I thought I could not bear to listen any longer. But I listened. Exhausted people were sleeping in the halls of the old hospital, the lucky ones on army cots, others on the dirt outside the brick building. A fifty-five-year-old mother put her hand on my shoulder. "Look, we're here six days, a family of five people, and we all sleep on one cot." A man pointed to a couple sound asleep on the dirt. "Look how they sleep," he said, "in the rain and in the hot sun. Soon it will be winter; they'll be sleeping this way in the snow." Barefoot children, covered with sores from the dirt and the lack of care, crowded around us. People were washing

New arrivals— barefoot, exhausted from their trek across rivers, mountains, and hazardous border crossings—rest on crowded makeshift beds outside the jammed Rothschild Hospital DP camp.

Some seek shelter along the walls and hedges of the hospital garden.

Others find respite from the sun sitting and standing under trees. I remind myself: this is Vienna, the fabled city of opera, wine gardens, and edelweiss.

The death camps have shaped them, given them the strength to fight the British Empire and demand justice. As we prepare to leave the Rothschild Hospital, the people burst into "Hatikvah," which means "hope."

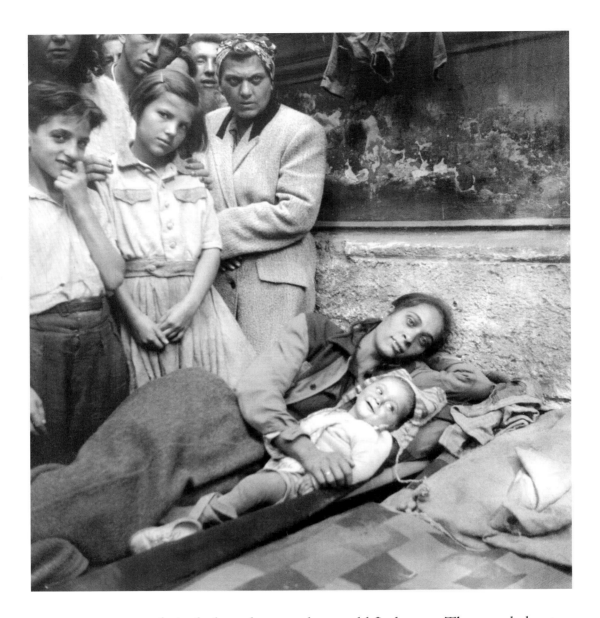

People ask us: Have you really come to help us? Or are you just another committee come to see what a DP looks like?

their clothes wherever they could find water. They needed water: water for drinking, bathing, laundry; water in the hope of preventing disease, to survive. Dr. Fabregat shook his head. "We have to end these conditions. We have to get these people out of here, to Palestine."

We were in Jerusalem listening to more speeches in the YMCA when I turned on my radio and learned that a refugee

A mother with a child can smile. She is beginning the task of replacing one of the 1.5 million children who were murdered. The childless woman next to the baby has dead eyes. She tells me her life is over.

A mother holding her child has regained hope: her baby has given her back her womanhood. But the children near her are still filled with despair.

Outside the hospital, they find water for drinking, cooking, bathing, and laundry. Cleanliness, they learned in the death camps, is the bulwark against lice and disease.

ALLENBY BRIDGE
POST
THE ARAB LEGION

At the border, Arab guards welcome me as the first journalist to enter the new Hashemite Kingdom of Jordan.

ship named *Exodus 1947* was attempting to break through the British blockade to enter Palestine.

I cabled the *Herald Tribune:* "Anybody can cover speeches. I'm going to cover a ship of refugees."

"Do it," the *Tribune* cabled back.

2

Haifa

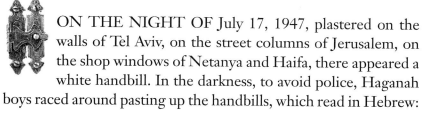 ON THE NIGHT OF July 17, 1947, plastered on the walls of Tel Aviv, on the street columns of Jerusalem, on the shop windows of Netanya and Haifa, there appeared a white handbill. In the darkness, to avoid police, Haganah boys raced around pasting up the handbills, which read in Hebrew:

The refugee ship called *Exodus 1947* is headed for the shores of Palestine, after having succeeded in breaking through the blockade upon emigration from ports of exit.

The Haganah ship *Exodus 1947* has 4,554 refugees:

> 1,600 men
> 1,282 women
> 1,017 young people
> 655 children

The ship has been spotted by the British navy. A naval force, five destroyers and a cruiser, are now closing in on her from all sides, and leading her on her way.

At 22 hours tonight, and tomorrow morning at 7:30, the refugees will broadcast a message to the Jews of Palestine from the deck of the ship on 35 meters wavelength. The broadcast may be picked up on the Haganah secret radio, Kol Israel [The Voice of Israel], 45 meters wavelength.

Shortly after dawn, a voice came over *The Voice of Israel*, a voice with an American accent. It was the voice of an American student-preacher, John Stanley Grauel, and he spoke urgently.

"This is the refugee ship Exodus 1947. *Before dawn today we were attacked by five British destroyers and one cruiser at a distance of seventeen miles from the shores of Palestine, in international waters. The assailants immediately opened fire, threw gas bombs, and rammed our ship from three directions. On our deck there are one dead, five dying, and a hundred twenty wounded. The resistance continued for more than three hours. Owing to the severe losses and the condition of the ship, which is in danger of sinking, we were compelled to sail in the direction of Haifa, in order to save the forty-five hundred refugees on board from drowning."*

On Friday, July 18, the city of Tel Aviv shut down. The citizens closed their shops and restaurants voluntarily; turned off the machinery in the factories, and halted their whole economy to protest to the world.

The strike was the explosive culmination of the citizens' resentment. The last survivors of their families were still living in the DP camps in Germany, in the death land. The citizens of Tel Aviv had decided to defy the British, who were barring the Jews from Palestine, and by means of Haganah, their Army of Resistance, they had begun to run their relatives and thousands of unknown DPs through the British blockade. The *Exodus 1947*, now approaching, was the largest refugee ship to date to attempt the illegal landing, and she had already been caught and crushed.

"You won't let our people land" became the battle slogan of the strikers of Tel Aviv. Each shopkeeper passed this slogan on to his neighbor, each factory manager to his workers, and by ten o'clock on that fateful Friday morning, Tel Aviv, the largest all-Jewish city in the world, with over 200,000 people, bustling, active, clean, ambitious, adolescent, full of destiny and vinegar—a Beverly Hills on the Mediterranean—had willingly stopped breathing.

I walked through the crowds. The air was electric with indignation. Conjecture and fear steamed up like the heat from the sidewalk: "Maybe my father is on board"; "My sister must surely be coming"; "My son said he would be in the very next sailing."

Tel Aviv looked like a dinosaur that had frozen in its tracks. Buses stopped dead in the middle of the road. I walked past my hotel, which overlooked the Mediterranean. A flag was raised on the white beach, informing the people that there was to be no swimming. Only a short while before, the best-dressed women and men in Palestine had been eating breakfast on gay verandas. Now all the fashionable hotels were blacked out, their chairs pulled in, and their shutters pulled down.

On Allenby Road, two British tanks, hugging each other for protection, crawled slowly down the street, apparently looking for trouble. They found it. Hundreds of men and women yelling, "There's a strike on. You won't let our people land. No vehicle moves!" rushed into the gutters and in front of the tanks. The tanks stopped. A young soldier crawled up through a hatchway and stood in the turret. His voice, as he called into his walkie-talkie for help, was staccato with fear.

At another corner, a bearded Arab drove a horse and wagon through an intersection. In the wagon sat his little son and his wife, veiled to the eyes. A crowd of boys rushed noisily toward the wagon, grabbed hold of the horse's head, and began to move the wagon backward. A few older Jewish men dragged the boys away and, with apologies, told the Arab, in Arabic, to drive on. "We're not fighting the Arabs," one of the men explained to the frustrated boys, "we're fighting the British."

The car in which a good friend was to drive me the sixty-seven miles to Haifa was parked outside the hotel. We decided that if we were to reach the port in time to see the ship come in, we would have to leave immediately. We pasted our huge PRESS sign across the windshield and drove as slowly as the armored tanks through the milling streets. It was worse than breaking through a picket line. This was defying the will of a whole people; there were no strike-breakers in Tel Aviv. We felt sacrilegious, as though we were break-ing a holy vow. The only excuse we could give our guilty consciences was that we were trying to reach the ship for which the people had paralyzed their city. We had to repeat that excuse to var-ious men and women who stopped us at street corners, demanding to know whether we knew there was a strike on. We said we knew. We also said the *Exodus 1947* was already on the horizon.

The port of Naples had been less guarded in the wartime summer of 1944 than Haifa was now in the summer of 1947. Great coils of rusted wire ran all over the pier. Tanks, trucks, jeeps, military police, secret police, the constabulary, CID (Criminal Investigation Department) men, and about five hundred gunners from the artillery branch of the 6th Airborne Division filled the waterfront. MPs checked us constantly at barbed-wire checking posts.

The heroes of El Alamein and Tobruk were waiting for the enemy. They were the red-bereted gunners of the airborne division who carried through the operation of getting the people off the illegal ships. They were young; their bodies were lithe with army calisthenics; their faces were like the faces of men before H hour on D-Day.

Their commanding officer, Major Cardozo, wore a summer battle jacket with two rows of battle ribbons pinned across his left breast. He was a short man, who stretched himself for height. His back was as straight as a firing wall; he had a suspicious trace of a stomach, which he studiously sucked in. He never walked: he danced.

While he waltzed across the cluttered pier, he twirled his stick like a drum majorette. For the most part, a pleased smile played on his face. It was a soft, almost infantile face, with soft, babylike lips, a soft double chin, and amazingly cold blue eyes. He looked like a man who knew that this was a big show, maybe the biggest peacetime circus he would ever participate in, and that destiny had chosen him to be the ringside barker. He told me he was related to the Cardozo family that is famous in the United States; that his family had been expelled from Spain during the Inquisition, had moved to Holland, had been persecuted there after becoming Catholics, and had finally gone to England.

The major permitted no one in the port of Haifa except the army, the navy, and the assorted press of the world, busy at the moment covering the hearings of the United Nations Special Committee on Palestine. Every fishing boat in the harbor seemed to be

Major Cardozo of the British 6th Airborne Division, in charge of getting the 4,500 refugees off the Exodus 1947 *in Haifa, grins for the camera. He knows this is a historic day. Destiny has chosen him to strut upon the stage. He does not walk; he dances on the pier.*

holding its breath. Tied up against a pier was the *Ocean Vigour,* one of the caged prison ships in which the people were to be transported to Cyprus, we thought. Against another pier were two other prison ships, the *Runnymede Park* and the *Empire Rival.*

The pier was cluttered and confused. Tracks ran down its middle, as in a railroad yard. A kind of steel *arc de triomphe,* wheeled to the tracks, supported a movable crane. A pile of savage-looking Sten guns lay on top of one another on hospital stretchers, as though cause and effect had been confused already, and soon the men and women wounded by these guns would be lying on these very stretchers.

The newspaper people were kept on the pier, with the soldiers standing like a wall between us and the dock where the ship was to berth. Only the photographers and newsreel men were allowed to climb the steel arch to get closer to the people. Major Cardozo warned us that anyone caught talking to the refugees would be expelled immediately.

He kept prancing up and down, throwing us bits of information. "The biggest load we've ever gotten in here," he said. "The fight began at four A.M. this morning . . . inside territorial waters." He made a point of that . . . "inside territorial waters." "Many wounded . . . they claim three dead. They rammed the ship first . . . they resisted."

His friendliness, whenever he stayed long enough in one place, made it possible to ask him questions. We all knew, because everyone said it and because it was the pattern, that these people would be taken to Cyprus. "What's it like on those prison ships?" I wanted to know, pointing to the *Ocean Vigour* and the *Runnymede Park*. "Will you let us go aboard?"

"Oh no, no, no. You can't go aboard. But conditions are fine. Fine. Beds. Plenty of food. Water, all they want to drink. Not the *Queen Mary*, you understand. But decent, with everything they need to make them comfortable until they get to Cyprus. Sorry you can't see it, but take my word, conditions are much better than on those frightful ships they came to Palestine in."

I was to remember this conversation later, in southern France.

On the skyline, the *Exodus* rode the edge of a rough sea. She seemed to be marching through the water like a prisoner surrounded by troops. Ahead was the famous cruiser *Ajax*, all 6,985 tons of her, proud of all the Nazi ships she had under her belt. Behind was a row of destroyers.

Shortly before four in the afternoon, operations began. His Majesty's Royal Navy fixed their steel helmets. The Royal

Marines hitched up their pants. The gunners and paratroopers, in full battle dress, stood at their battle stations. The *Ajax* and the destroyers remained outside the harbor.

The enemy came in slowly, a black, shabby, broken steamer, pulled into place by British tugs. She had a single tall black funnel. Fore and aft, the blue-and-white flag of Zion flew from her masts. We saw her name clearly now:

HAGANAH SHIP

Exodus 1947

The voices of thousands of people floated to us on the quay. They were singing "Hatikvah," the Hebrew hymn of hope. It was the song the Jews sang at every emergency and in every crisis. It was their song of survival.

The ship looked like a matchbox that had been splintered by a nutcracker. In the torn, square hole, as big as an open, blitzed barn, we could see a muddle of bedding, possessions, plumbing, broken pipes, overflowing toilets, half-naked men, women looking for children. Cabins were bashed in; railings were ripped off; the lifesaving rafts were dangling at crazy angles.

Framed in the smashed deck stood a blond man, with the saddest eyes I had ever seen. His whole life seemed to be in his eyes, sunk deep under his blond, almost colorless brows. He wore no tie; his ragged trousers were rolled above his bare ankles; his torn shirt was open; his arms were stretched out, holding on to two broken cables. He was Mordecai Rosman, a leader of the *Exodus*.

Up on the bridge were the British marines and sailors who had captured the vessel. The head of one of the marines was swathed in bandages. "That's a real iron-head up there," one of the British officers near me told another officer who was apparently new in the game. "He's always the first one to board these illegal ships and the first one off. Tough as iron. Always comes down with his eyes black, his nose bleeding, or his head bandaged. But nothing seems to hurt him." The second officer laughed admiringly.

From somewhere on the dock, a loudspeaker began to address the people, who now crowded every hole and porthole on our

The battered Exodus, *with its tall black smokestack, flying the blue-and-white flag of Zion, with the Star of David on it, limps into Haifa. The voices of the people on the ship defiantly singing "Hatikvah" float down to us on the dock.*

Earlier, in the battle at sea, British soldiers and marines board the Exodus *with tear gas, guns, helmets, and truncheons. The refugees fight back with canned food, potatoes, and sticks. For the children, the gunfire, and the tear gas burning their throats and eyes, are terrifying. Bill Bernstein of San Francisco, one of the most beloved officers on the ship, tries to keep the British out of the wheelhouse where he's been steering the ship. A marine kills him with a blow to the skull. Other marines kill two teenage orphans. At least 150 refugees and crew are wounded.*

Exodus 1947 *comes to a halt where I am standing. British destroyers have rammed her from both sides, turning the walls of the promenade deck into rubble. Amazingly, she does not break apart. The Exodus looks like a matchbox splintered by a nutcracker.*

The white Ocean Vigour, *at right, a Lend-Lease ship the United States had sent to help save Britain during World War II, waits in the harbor for the* Exodus *to dock. Major Cardozo tells me the* Ocean Vigour *is a "hospital ship" fully equipped with beds and toilets, and milk for mothers and children. Later, in southern France, when I finally board one of the prison ships, I remember his words. Two other Lend-Lease ships, renamed the* Empire Rival *and the* Runnymede Park, *stand ready nearby. Cardozo says that the three ships will take the 4,500 Jews of the* Exodus *to the British internment camps on the island of Cyprus. Instead they are taken to France and then to Germany.*

The man in the white shirt, standing amid the rubble at the upper left, is Mordecai Rosman, one of the most passionate and courageous leaders of the refugees, and one of the last to disembark.

The refugees finally come off the ship and step on the land they have dreamed of for so long. They are sprayed with DDT powder and immediately transferred onto one of the three ships supposedly bound for Cyprus.

side. The loudspeaker said in Hebrew, "The commanding officer wishes you to come off quietly, women and children first."

Soldiers placed gangways into the holes and then ran up to take charge. Several stretchers were carried aboard. The first person to come down was a pale, sick woman, holding the arm of her husband. She wore a huge army raincoat that made her look like a scarecrow. She carried no bundles, no bags at all. Her face was white and sunken; her eyes were sunken; her lips trembled. She looked like a thousand years of misery.

"Big Bill" Millman, who had served aboard the cruiser U.S.S. Pittsburgh *in World War II and won a boxing championship, is shot in the jaw by a British marine while trying to retake the wheelhouse. Writhing in pain, Bill is carried by British soldiers to an ambulance that will take him to a hospital in Haifa.*

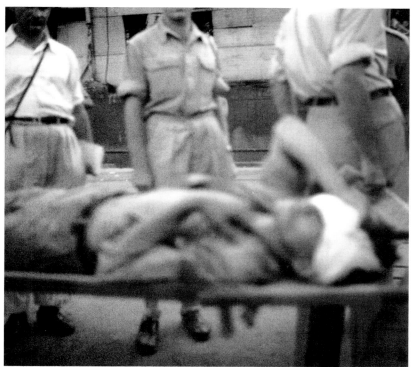

Nat Nadler, a Brooklyn-born electrician, and Bill Millman's friend, is bludgeoned over his right eye during the battle and knocked unconscious. A refugee doctor sews up the wound. On the dock, British medics pull the bandage off his head and say his wounds are not serious, forcing him off the gurney and making him walk to the Ocean Vigour.

The DPs' worldly belongings line the pier. The British assure the refugees they will get their belongings back on Cyprus.

A child came off, with large, frightened eyes. He carried a potato sack with his belongings; a blanket was strapped across his back. A man and a child came down, hand in hand. The child broke away and ran back up the gangway, looking for his mother. He was sobbing with fright. The soldiers gently pulled him down the gangway again. No one was allowed to return to the ship.

A man with the dark look of hunger came down, carrying a briefcase. A cigarette dipped out of the side of his mouth. Soldiers followed, carrying the dead body of a sixteen-year-old orphan, Hirsch Yakubovich, who had come from the DP orphanage in

Kloster-Indersdorf, Bavaria. He had been killed in the battle. The soldiers then brought down the American second mate, Bill Bernstein, mortally wounded. He was unconscious; his head was hidden in bandages. His thin body was dressed in army shorts; one knee was raised on the stretcher with the easy grace of a child asleep.

The people trickled down the gangways in little groups and milled on the dock like frightened animals. They looked weary and shattered, mourning their dead and hundreds wounded. Surrounded by the troops to prevent their escaping into Haifa, they made their first step on the dreamed-of soil. They breathed the air deeply and tiredly.

Still waiting on the ship, behind the confusion of bedding and baggage and splinters, other people stared out at the British. Some of their faces looked defiant; some were filled with hate; some of the people just stood like tourists.

For a little while, no one came off the ship. I learned later that the soldiers were afraid that the Jews would not disembark peacefully. The soldiers told the refugees that the *Ocean Vigour*, the first of the transports, was a hospital ship with milk for mothers and children. Most of the sick and the families went down to be put on the "hospital ship," or to be taken to the hospital at Haifa.

On the pier, the British took off every bandage and examined every wound to make sure that only the serious cases stayed. Some of the wounded screamed with pain as their head dressings were untied and then tied up again. A military ambulance waited on the dock. When the army doctor nodded his head, a patient was placed on one of the ambulance gurneys, while the refugees and the American crewmen, who had now disguised themselves as refugees, watched the lottery. To be sent to Haifa's hospitals, they had to belong more to the dead than to the living.

Inside the ship that once had carried excursionists up and down the Chesapeake, soldiers gave the 4,500 refugees a mimeographed statement in several languages which told them that they were going to Cyprus and that they would get their baggage there. "Have you got your stickers?" the troops kept asking the people, handing them big parcel-post stickers on which to put their names. The soldiers assured them that if the baggage was properly labeled, it would be returned to them tomorrow in Cyprus.

The slow march down the gangplanks started again. A woman with large green eyes and the high cheekbones of a Hungarian beauty came down precipitously, wheeling a straw baby carriage. In it was a three-year-old baby with the same facial structure, the gypsylike eyes and skin.

A group of adolescent Hungarian girls came down and giggled. Almost everyone carried a big green bottle of water. This was the mark of the illegal refugee, his or her water bottle. There never was enough drinking water; each person on the underground route to Palestine carried his own bottle with him. It was

The walking wounded are aided by British medics.

the first thing the British soldiers took away, as though it were a secret weapon. The pier, near the customs table, was littered with broken glass, as the British dashed each bottle into splinters.

The long journey from the riverboat to the prison boat began. The refugees walked inside the tracks lined with soldiers under the British *arc de triomphe*. First their hand baggage was thoroughly searched at a long table by soldiers of the 6th Airborne Division and the CID. All scissors, knives, razors, and fountain pens, which might be used as weapons, were confiscated. These were never returned. Films were taken out of their cameras and their cameras were taken away.

A severely wounded refugee is helped by a kindly soldier and a friend.

A group of young Hungarian girls comes off the ship giggling: Erika Klein at left, her face half-hidden, her sister Rachel, and next to her is Lea Snitzer. Despite everything, this is somehow still a great adventure for the girls.

Each refugee has carried a green bottle of water on the Exodus. *It is the first thing the British seize and smash on the wharf. After that, they confiscate all sharp objects— knives, pens, even cameras—anything the refugees might use to win their freedom.*

Only a few had identity cards, but some still had UNRRA cards, saying they had been displaced persons at Feldafing, or Landsberg, or some other DP camp in Germany. All their identity cards were taken. A man whispered to me furtively. I hoped he was going to tell me in a few words what had happened, words stolen through the cordon of guards. But he was telling me the most important fact in his life: that his mother lived right up there on Mount Carmel. Would I please let her know right away that her son had arrived on the *Exodus*, was safe, would write her from Cyprus? Then he lost all fear and kept shouting the address, until the British came and dragged him away.

The reporter for *Davar* attempted to talk to someone in a little space along the tracks where, for a moment, there was no soldier. But Major Cardozo, quick as ever, caught the act, forgot his dignity and his stick, ran to the newspaperman, and grabbed his arm. His baby face boiled lobster red. He called two MPs, ordered them to take the newspaperman off the dock immediately, and gave strict instructions to every MP at the gates that this man was not, under any circumstances, to be allowed on the pier again.

The heat grew worse. The soldiers wilted; cigarettes hung listlessly from the sides of their mouths. The pier began to take on the noise and smell and animal tragedy of a Chicago slaughterhouse. The cattle moved slowly down the tracks.

There were new faces in the track under the *arc de triomphe*, and new DP types, but the expressions began to fuse into one face of weariness and despair. The agony which had begun for them with the war was being dragged on for another historic day, to be placed in their minds with the days of occupation, the day of liberation, and now the long-awaited day of arrival in the Holy Land.

The little children continued to look solemn and silent and old, as though they had never known any world but this one and they could take it in their stride. But the older people began to show panic as they looked at the mounting piles of duffel bags, potato sacks, paper suitcases, and knapsacks in which they had packed all their worldly goods. They kept pointing to the pile, begging the soldiers to let them find their belongings. The soldiers moved them along.

On the ship, soldiers tossed the baggage out of the portholes. A loud, anguished cry went up as one of the bags missed the pile and dropped forever into the sea.

Depth bombs kept exploding. The British were making sure there were no underwater swimmers to sabotage their work. Major Cardozo danced back and forth. The hot sun beat unmercifully, and the refugees, wearing all they could rescue on their backs, stood drenched in sweat. They mopped their faces with dirty hands and waited to be taken on board the prison ships. No one cried. No one complained. Some walked slowly, dragging their feet, like people in a dream.

The refugees looked up at Mount Carmel and seemed to say to themselves, *This land is mine. Soon it will be mine forever. They're only taking us to Cyprus. We'll be there only a year or two. Then we'll come back with visas. We'll come back forever.*

Inside the unreality, there were two realities, family and be-longings. The family might not even be a blood family; it might be a family made in the concentration camp, or a family collected together on the road or at the borders which the long exodus crossed. But whether it was a made family or a blood family, they were terrified at losing it. And now terror struck.

The people were being separated by the soldiers, men from women, into "search pens," lean-tos made of walls of brown sackcloth and strips of wood. In their unreal world, separation meant only one thing—death. They had been separated in their towns by the SS, and that had meant deportation and shooting. They had been separated in Auschwitz, Dachau, and Treblinka by the Nazi soldiers, and that had meant the gas chambers. Now they were being separated again. Some screamed; some tried to fight off the soldiers; some clung to their families. But they were separated anyway, gently for the most part, but sometimes crudely, depending on the soldier or policeman at work.

Four Arab women, one of them with a big hole in the heel of her black-cotton stockings, searched the women's bodies. We were not allowed to watch the operation in the search pen, but the reputation of the policewomen in Haifa was not good.

The men were searched in a separate sackcloth pen by soldiers and police. They came out of the lean-tos buttoning up their pants. A few smirked a little, as if they had been caught coming out of a bawdy house.

The separation and the terror it evoked continued as they were marched farther along the track to the DDT pens. It was the era of DDT, of death to everything that crawled. Soldiers sprayed the flourlike powder on their hair, down their shirts, up their trousers and skirts, and all over their legs.

By this time the heat had become suffocating. The babies, who had been incredibly quiet, began to cry. Men looked dazed and ready to collapse as the red-bereted soldiers shoved them along the last mile. Members of families, separated for the search pens, were taken to different transports. They were reassured that they would be reunited the next day in Cyprus.

Night was infinitely worse on the broken and defeated *Exodus* than day; fatigued and hungry, most of the people gave up the ship. Hundreds came off in a great spurt and waited, pressed hotly against one another on one end of the wharf. The soldiers kept carrying fainting men and pregnant women to a dimly lit first-aid army tent at the entrance of the dock. The people were given treatment and then marched down the processing tracks between two soldiers.

I left the dock to file a story and returned at midnight. The character of the wharf had changed, and even the character of the people seemed different. Their eyes were turned inward now. They had stopped staring up at Mount Carmel. Glaring blue and green searchlights played weirdly on the nameless brooding mass of people and on the wounded boat that would soon be pulled around to the graveyard of illegal ships.

The eerie lights picked up bits of the people's bodies, bare feet, torn clothes, bandaged arms and heads, faces oily with sweat and dark with resentment and mourning. These last to leave the *Exodus* were the fighters, the philosophers, the ideologists, the leaders, the ones who clung most desperately to the ship and the hope they knew was hopeless—that maybe they could stay.

It was easier to talk to the people now, but they were too hungry to say much. They had eaten nothing for almost thirty hours, since their supper at seven the night before.

The battle was over; for some it had ended at nine, when the *Ocean Vigour,* the "hospital ship," had finished loading and departed. The next group to accept defeat had gone out on the *Runnymede Park,* and at five-forty in the morning, the last of the *Exodus* people sailed on the *Empire Rival.*

Only the broken hull of the excursion boat remained at the dock, with a few soldiers to guard it in its loneliness.

• • •

Back in the press-corralled bar of the Savoy Hotel, the American student-preacher, who had traveled as an ordinary seaman on the ship and served as cook's helper, gave us the story of the battle. An American flag was sewn onto the shirtsleeve of his left arm.

The shirt, a soiled khaki color, was flung open; a delicate cross hung on his bare chest. He was bronzed from the sun; blood lines ran through his large blue eyes. His blond hair fell across his forehead and was combed long at the sides and back, like the hair of a Puritan. There was something romantically adolescent about him, and though he was twenty-nine, I could as readily have believed he was nineteen. He told us he was John Stanley Grauel from Worcester, Massachusetts, correspondent for The Churchman and a member of the American Christian Palestine Committee. It was he who had spoken on The Voice of Israel from the Exodus in the morning. We recognized his New England accent.

He talked with the excitement and gasping strength of a man who has run off the battlefield with the first eyewitness account. He started with jumbled phrases; then his words became smoother; he began to see the story again, the story of the strange naval battle between a once elegant little steamer and five destroyers and the *Ajax*.

The *Exodus* story had begun in America, for the ship was an American excursion boat and the crew were GIs and sailors and merchant-marine men.

Her life had been structured, like a classic play, into three acts. Act one began on a carnival note when her keel was laid in Wilmington, Delaware, in September 1927. She was the flagship of the Old Bay Line, and one of the last of the small inland steamers carrying 400 excursioners, honeymooners, gamblers, businesspeople and fun-lovers on nightly rides from Baltimore to Norfolk, along the Chesapeake Bay.

Painted a festive white, with romantic balconies, staterooms for distinguished guests, especially from the Old South, and an elegant ballroom, she was the creation of a wealthy Baltimorean named Solomon Davies Warfield. He was president of a railroad line and a steamship company, and the uncle of the Duchess of Windsor, Wallace Warfield Simpson, the American "woman I love" for whom King Edward VIII gave up his throne. Warfield died just before the ship was launched. In his honor, the ship was named the *President Warfield*.

Act two opened solemnly in World War II. In 1942, painted battle gray and outfitted with gun tubs, the little inland steamer was transferred to the British Ministry, sailing under British registry and the red British flag, an irony that would later appear in act three. Traveling in a convoy of large, majestic ships, dodging Nazi U-boats, she braved the waves of the Atlantic. She took part in the D-Day invasion, unloading supplies and ammunition on the Normandy beachhead.

In act three she returned home to Baltimore ready for the scrap heap, but sprang back to life in November 1946, bought for forty thousand dollars by American Friends of the Haganah, the Jewish Army of Resistance. She was to enter history, moving Jews out of Europe on the route they called Aliyah Beth. It meant immigration, the going up. She became the largest ship thus far in the secret fleet carrying refugees determined to reach Palestine. Almost within sight of the coast of the Holy Land, her crew painted the sign that read:

HAGANAH SHIP
Exodus 1947

They named her the *Exodus 1947*, for they guessed that she might take her place in history with the other great exoduses of Jews.

The crew had signed up in protest, indignant that Jews who had lost six million dead were still living in the degradation of DP camps, barred by the British from Palestine.

The thirty-five American crewmen served under a handful of Palestinian Jews, who had been rigorously trained in the rescue of Jews by both the Palmach, the military arm, and the Palyam, the naval arm, of the Haganah. The Palyam men tried to impress upon the Americans the need for secrecy. They treated secrecy as if it were a holy vow. Whenever they were in port, knowing the British had agents everywhere and the boys might imbibe too much, the Palyamniks put their fingers to their lips and whispered, "Hush up." The Americans found this hilarious and soon dubbed the Palestinians the "shoo-shoo boys."

The captain of the *Exodus* was Ike Aronowitz, a small, wiry twenty-two-year-old who looked like a teenager. He had the air of a street-smart youngster well schooled in sailing. He had left Poland as a child and at sixteen joined Palyam's first class, as it established its navy. He began to sail on cargo ships, and then, in London, studied in a maritime college. He was twenty-one when he was made a third mate in the British merchant marine. In London too, he met Shaul Avigur, the head of Aliyah Beth, who was so impressed that he chose Ike to be master of the *Exodus*. Ike was startled, but he vowed he would bring the 4,500 survivors home to Eretz Israel. His identity was kept top secret to prevent the British from arresting him for sailing this so-called illegal ship.

Yossi Harel was a large, impressive man, a presence on the ship as he walked the decks, representing the Mossad, Israel's nascent secret service. Years later he helped capture Adolf Eichmann in Argentina. He came aboard the *Exodus* in Portovenere, Italy, and served as a kind of commandant and coach, making policy, giving inspirational talks on the public-address system, keeping the refugees informed on how far along they were in their perilous voyage. At twenty-nine, he was an old hand in smuggling refugees into Palestine. He had already sailed on another of the illegal ships, and had fought the British sailors who captured him and sent him to Cyprus.

On July 10, 1947, the morning after 4,500 refugees had climbed aboard the ship in Sète in southern France, to begin their journey, Yossi greeted them on the public-address system. "My dear brothers and sisters, this day is without doubt a great day for all of us. Today we've managed to send four thousand five hundred Jews to Eretz Israel. Our ship is the largest immigrant ship in the history of the Zionist movement."

He then introduced the Palestinian Jews by the code names they had assumed in case they were captured. Yossi himself was Amnon. Captain Ike's real name was Yitzchak, but his code name Ike was so fitting that to this day he has no other name. Each of the escort team had not only code names but specific roles. Tsvi

Katsenelson, code name Miri, was in charge of food and water. Micha Perry, code name Gad, was in charge of discipline, security, and preparing the people for the battle they were sure would come. Azriel Enaf, code name Barak, was in charge of communicating both with Jerusalem and with the Mossad's offices in Europe. He controlled the public-address system on the ship. The most beloved member of the team was known by her first name, Sima. She was Sima Schmucker, a warm, compassionate woman, responsible for all the health services, and especially for the care of the pregnant women and children. During the battle at sea, she never left the deck, working closely with Dr. Cohen, chief of the refugee doctors, binding heads, applying salve to burn victims, and comforting some of the terrified children.

Four of the Palestinians had done the regular underground run three or four times in the previous ten months. One of them was a young girl who was making the run for the first time and who was later to distinguish herself in the Israeli army as a combat officer.

On the public-address system, Yossi introduced the American crew to the refugees. "The ship's contingent of sailors and workers," he said, "are all young Jews from America who left everything behind and volunteered, not to get any prizes, but to bring Jews to Eretz Israel."

The American chief officer, the ship's first mate, was twenty-four-year-old Bernard Marks from Cincinnati. Tall and thin, looking like a college basketball player, Bernie was a soft-spoken, unassuming, brilliant seaman, an almost saintly role model for the American crew. He was a member of the Masters, Mates and Pilots Union, with master's papers. He had already served on an Aliyah Beth ship and was well aware of the dangers, as British destroyers trailed the *Exodus.*

The second mate was Bill Bernstein, twenty-three, born in Passaic, New Jersey, where he attended public school, moved to Brooklyn, then to San Francisco, where he refused the deferment in World War II offered him as a premedical student. He graduated from the U.S. Merchant Marine Academy at Kings Point in Long Island, and then became an ensign in the U.S.

Navy. Red-haired, smiling, sensitive, Bill was the most popular man in the crew.

The third mate, Cyril Weinstein, from Brooklyn, had a game leg from infantile paralysis and the enormous shoulder and chest strength of compensation. He was tall and broad, with a Roosevelt-like quality about his open face, his big jaw, and his easy smile. He had studied sculpture at the Art Students League in New York after he finished serving in the merchant marine during the war. Cy was twenty-two.

Then there was Dov Miller, twenty-two, from Brooklyn, a born leader and a veteran of Okinawa, who had been a Zionist most of his life. There were others who had never been interested in Jews until Hitler murdered most of them and the British barred the rest from going home.

In January 1947, the American boys assembled in Baltimore, where the refurbished steamer had been outfitted for her ocean crossing. On February 25, friends of the Haganah came down from Washington and New York. A silk flag of Zion was presented to the ship, someone gave each crew member a sweater, a Bible, and some books, and the *President Warfield* set sail for Europe.

In mid-Atlantic, she ran into a hurricane which battered her so badly that the boys sent out an SOS. A U.S. Coast Guard vessel escorted her back to America under her own steam. Once more they worked on the ship, and then set out again. They learned that the British Foreign Office had set up a special espionage office called Illegal Jewish Immigration (IJI) and had flung a network of agents around the globe to halt the march to Palestine. In the Azores, the boys heard that the British had warned the Portuguese port authorities against selling them fuel or water. The crew managed to get both, and sailed to Marseille, trying to outwit the British. They moved on to the picturesque harbor town of Port-de-Bouc and stayed there until they decided to go to Italy to take much of the ship apart and prepare it physically for its ultimate goal.

"Our plan," Bernie Marks explained to me more than fifty years later, "was to sail far south, just north of Egypt, then turn north, staying just beyond Palestinian waters—always staying in international waters until we came abreast of Tel Aviv. Tel Aviv is known for its gentle sloping beach. Then we would turn hard to starboard in a dash to beach her."

The plan was for the Palmach to have hundreds of people on the beach, speeding the refugees off the ship and dispersing them throughout the city as if they were all Tel Avivians. They felt good about their plan.

In Italy, they dropped anchor in Portovenere, the beautiful harbor near La Spezia, where they stripped the ship to bare essentials, sold everything they didn't need, and built wooden bunks wherever there was space. Some of the shelves were five and six feet high, like the wooden bunks in the death camps, but no one complained. These bunks were for life, not death.

Bevin was unrelenting. He brought pressure on the Italian government to halt the march to Palestine. One night an Italian navy cable tender that looked to the crew like a gunboat dropped its anchor across their bows. They were stymied, convinced the Italians would fire on them if they moved.

They spent seven weeks in the Italian port, four of them without shore leave. Each day Italian girls would row out to the riverboat and tease the boys who hung over the sides. The crew was sure the Italian girls were the most beautiful girls in the world. It was Bill Bernstein who saved them from going mad from boredom. Each night Bill put on a show. His favorite act was a takeoff on Harpo Marx; he used a floor mop for hair.

While they were trapped in Portovenere, a woman was fighting for their release. She was Ada Sereni, a small forty-year-old Italian Jewish beauty who was in charge of all the Aliyah Beth operations in Italy. Ada was the widow of Enzio Sereni, one of Italy's beloved heroes, who had parachuted behind the Nazi lines and was caught, tortured, and killed. In gratitude for her husband's bravery, the Italians were prepared to do whatever she requested. It took time, but finally the cable tender moved enough to let the *President Warfield* slip through.

They sailed to Marseille to pick up oil and install the wooden bunks they had built in Italy. From there they moved back to

Port-de-Bouc, spent about a week there preparing the ship for its hazardous voyage through the British blockade, and then sailed to Sète.

July 10 was D-Day. "You should have seen the line of trucks coming down the road," Nat Nadler, the ship's electrician, told me. "They were coming from DP camps all over Europe like army trucks rendezvousing before a battle. I'll never forget that sight."

From early morning to evening, they loaded the passengers: 4,500 people who had come from all parts of Europe, from the DP camps of Germany, from Poland and Hungary and Romania, from Belgium and France and Italy, and even from Morocco— Jews who were determined to quit Europe and the memory of Hitlerism forever.

But Ernest Bevin, Britain's foreign secretary, had dedicated himself to stopping the *Exodus*. The boys learned that in Paris he had told French Foreign Minister Bidault that the *Exodus* must be held in port; under no circumstance was she to be allowed to leave the harbor.

The crew discovered too that on the next day the French, under pressure, intended to impound their ship and had threatened to arrest any French pilot who helped them. It was tonight or never. They bribed a pilot with a million francs. He told them he would try to come; if he was not there by 2:00 A.M., then he would not come at all.

The boys sat up in the Palestinian captain's cabin, drinking coffee, pacing the deck, and watching for the French pilot. Could they risk taking the ship out without a pilot and tugboats? At 1:30 A.M., Bernie Marks, the American first mate, stripped to his underwear, jumped off the ship, swam through the dark water, and unfastened all but one cable and one hawser. He returned to the ship. At 10:00 A.M., when it was certain that the French pilot was not coming, the boys raised anchor. They broke three fire axes trying to cut the steel cable aft.

"On Friday, July eleventh," Bernie Marks, the first mate, told me, "we had to leave without benefit of tug or pilot, because the French pilot had gone back on his word."

Getting a 330-foot-long ship out of a harbor almost the same size without a tugboat or pilot seemed almost impossible. They tried to make a right turn and failed. They backed into the seawall too hard. Pulling away, they got stuck twice in a mud bank. They rocked the ship repeatedly, broke free, and finally steamed through the channel.

Out in the Mediterranean, an unwelcome escort waited. His Majesty's Ship *Mermaid*, a frigate, patrolled the beat outside the harbor like a huge policeman on a dark night. The *Mermaid* immediately took up the trail. New destroyers came almost every day and joined the chase. Ships came from Malta and other bases in the Mediterranean, relieving each other regularly, like a major task force. The *Exodus* was a hare playing with a pack of wolfhounds, and even enjoying the hunt. When the wolfhounds came close, the Americans sang "The Yanks Are Coming" across their public-address system. "Pomp and Circumstance," dear to the hearts of the British, became the ship's commercial whenever a destroyer came alongside to check the *Exodus*'s speed and plan the offensive.

Sometimes the British, running close, told the passengers by megaphone:

"We suspect you are going to Palestine. It is illegal.

"If you enter Palestine, we will have to board you and arrest you.

"Please do not put up any resistance. We have overwhelming forces here and in Palestine to accomplish our mission. If necessary, we will use force to board you, but you will have medical attention."

The Americans found that last line the funniest: a humanitarian non sequitur. The boys were also amused when the British said, *"We have more forces at our disposal,"* as if the steamer might defeat the five destroyers and the British might have to bring up reserves. Sometimes on the ship itself, the answer was a strange noise known in greater New York as "the Bronx cheer." But the British did not hear it. The last two days, the crew decided to stop ignoring the British warnings. Then, with flags, they spelled two words, very simply: *Thank you*. It seemed to them like neat American irony.

Each night the American crew sat in one of the boys' cabins and discussed the battle that would come before they reached Haifa. "One of us," they would say, "is sure to get killed." Somebody said, "It ought to be Ritzer. He was in the marines. He still has lead in him from Guadalcanal. That would make a good story." Somebody disagreed. "No, it ought to be Bill Bernstein. He was an officer in the navy. That would really be something."

"I have a feeling it will be me," Bill said.

Nobody said anything.

It was during the voyage that the American crew began to learn more of the meaning of the exodus. They began to talk to the Jews. There was Sima Gaster, a twenty-six-year-old Polish girl whose husband had been burned in Auschwitz (the German name for the death camp in Oświęcim, Poland). She had fought as a partisan with the Red Army. There was a wealthy German burgher with a big mustache who came up on deck every day just in his undershirt, pants, and suspenders. He shepherded his wife and four children on the deck as if he were taking the family for a Sunday walk. There was Shmuel, a small, scholarly, quiet man, whose wife, Pola, expected another baby any day. She had refused to stay behind. "My baby shall be born in Eretz," she said, "in the Land of Israel."

There were pretty little girls with no parents who no longer wanted to stay in Europe with the Christian families who had hidden them. There was a little hunchback girl with sparkling black eyes, singled out by Harry Weinsaft, one of the American crew, who had himself been a refugee from Austria. Harry talked to the little deformed girl every day, knowing that his attentions would make her more popular among the other children.

One of the passengers told the Americans the story of the girl on another illegal ship, the Haganah ship *Hatikvah*. A British major had come on board after the British had captured the ship. The major asked if there was anyone who could speak English. He wanted to talk to someone in the captain's cabin. The people persuaded a tall, blond, beautiful girl of twenty-eight to go to him. She was reluctant, but she went at last. The major spoke very politely. "Tell me, what port did you sail from?"

She said to the major, "We sailed from Berlin."

"You're making fun of me," the major said. "It's illegal for you to leave Berlin and besides Berlin is a landlocked city. How could you sail from Berlin?"

"Major, did you ever read the Bible? Do you remember the story of how Moses took the children of Israel out of Egypt? He took them across the Red Sea. Only the Jews could cross. Major, we sailed from Berlin."

The major was angry. "What is your name, young woman?"

She pointed to her arm and read the numbers on it: "349821."

"What are you doing? I asked your name."

"I have no name. All these years I have had a number. I still have a number. Now I am going to Eretz Israel, to the Land of Israel, where I shall live as a Jew and a human being. Then I shall have a name."

The Americans learned more each day of the courage and the agony that had brought so many children and young people to the *Exodus*.

The ship had brought together three groups of people—the Palestinian Jews who commanded her, the Americans who sailed her, and the 4,500 survivors who squeezed together on the once elegant steamer built to hold 400.

• • •

Eight-year-old Uri Urmacher's odyssey was one of bereavement and terror. In 1939, he was caught in the Nazi blitzkrieg against his town of Siedlce near Warsaw. Fleeing with his parents and his little sister, Ruth, he sat huddled in a horse-drawn wagon while they crossed into Russia and continued to Uzbekistan, near the border with Afghanistan. Here his mother contracted cholera, and he was forbidden to touch her. When she died, he began to dream of her—holding her hand out to him, but never quite touching him. He woke up each night weeping.

His father, Shmuel, lived with a woman, who bore a child and then insisted that Uri and Ruth leave the house. They became, in effect, two orphans. In 1947, they were rescued by Haganah men and soldiers of the Jewish Brigade who had fought with the

British in Italy and who were searching for orphans, putting them on trains and trucks bound for ships that would take them to Palestine.

Uri and Ruth were settled in a cattle car called the "orphan car" bound for the first stage of their journey—Poland. Uri's father and companion managed to board one of the rear cars. One night, Uri, staring through the little window in a night-darkened forest, felt the train grind to a halt. His heart pounded as he saw Polish soldiers in uniform raise their guns. Bullets crashed through the train. The screams of frightened and dying children terrified him.

In the midst of the slaughter, Uri's father, together with the Haganah men, picked up an ax and raced through the train toward the engine room. Uri's father, holding the ax over the motorman's head, warned him, "If you don't get this train moving this minute, you'll never see daylight again."

The motorman, his hands trembling, sped away from the ambush. It was clear he was part of the conspiracy to kill the orphans, to prevent them from reclaiming the homes and the land their parents had owned before the war.

In Warsaw, the Haganah men transferred Uri and his sister along with the surviving orphans to another train, and then to a truck taking them to Marseille. They were placed in a huge, former French army camp, Grande Arenas. Here they were put in separate groups of thirty orphans their own age and shepherded aboard the *Exodus 1947*. Each group had its own leader, who stayed with them throughout the voyage, training them in the need for discipline to prevent chaos on the overcrowded little steamer.*

· · ·

For nine-year-old Bracha Rachmilewitz (born Bonbonica Budick), the journey from her home in Romania to the lower decks of the *Exodus* took two terrifying years. As a small child, she and her parents were sent by truck to a prison camp in Transnistria in the Romanian Ukraine, where over 120,000 Romanian Jews had been incarcerated. Within a few months, 70,000 were dead of

*After living on a kibbutz, Uri became an engineer on the Zim shipping lines. He moved to America, married Glenda Eiss, and is now a software specialist, testing computers that go into space.

hunger, typhus, and exposure to the freezing weather. Bracha was separated from her parents and put in the orphan barracks with thousands of other children, many of whom had been pulled from the arms of their mothers and fathers.

Liberated by the Russian army in 1945, Bracha was reunited with her parents and they began the journey to Palestine. Bracha, now an astonishingly beautiful child, could not read or write. In the years of running, she had never been to school. Always hungry, she would often weep with exhaustion. Her mother encouraged her to hold on. "Palestine," her mother comforted her, "is full of oranges. You love oranges. When we get there, you can have oranges every day." For Bracha, they were not traveling to the biblical land of milk and honey, but to the land of oranges.*

• • •

Fifteen-year-old Erika Klein Burger, who had been hidden during the war in a ghetto of Budapest and whose father had been murdered, made the journey from Hungary to the *Exodus* with her sister Rachel, her mother, and her grandmother. Arriving in Vienna on Christmas Eve 1945, Erika and Rachel were put into a group of two hundred children and taken to the DP camp in Leipheim, the former SS barracks between Stuttgart and Munich. There they were fed and clothed and even schooled by the American Jewish Joint Distribution Committee. In June 1947 they were put on a truck and taken to a camp in southern France, near Marseille.

"I finally boarded the *Exodus*," she wrote me later. "I felt very happy and thought our troubles were over. The fact that we had to sleep five girls to a bed—if you could call it a bed—did not bother me. The nights were terrible because of the extreme heat. But the truth is, the whole thing seemed to me like a big adventure—after all, we were only kids. We kept our Hebrew studies up. The main thing they asked of us [kids] was that we not run around the ship. Both my sister Rachel and my grandmother were on the ship with

*Bracha later studied medical science at the Hebrew University–Hadassah Medical School and became a hematology/oncology research scientist. She is the mother of three and has four grandchildren.

me and I was not afraid. We had very good leaders and they made sure that everything was taken care of for the group."*

• • •

Sara Wiener Kam, twenty, with large blue eyes and lustrous, shoulder-length blonde hair, was born in a small town in Poland named Belzyce, some twenty miles from Lublin. She grew up in a Zionist home and attended a Hebrew-speaking school. Her upper-middle-class family owned a mill, an oil press, part of a forest, and part of a small farm in a neighboring village named Chrzanów. In 1942 her father took her to Chrzanów and showed her where he had hidden a tin box filled with gold. The box was buried in the courtyard of a friendly Polish farmer. If she survived, he told her, the gold would be hers.

In 1942 the Gestapo deported most of Belzyce's 250 Jewish families and those in the surrounding towns. People who had hidden out were soon discovered and rounded up in a camp, where the Nazis first shot the elderly, then most of the men, women, and children, including Sara's mother and sister. The German soldiers counted out fifty strong young girls, obviously for slave labor, and sent them to a camp. Before the massacre, Sara had hidden in a cowshed for a few months, then, discovered or denounced, she was sent to a series of concentration camps: Belzyce; Budzin; Wieliczka; Auschwitz-Birkenau; and Taucha, near Leipzig. From Taucha she was taken on a death march by the Nazi guards fleeing the Russian advance. A few days before the war ended on May 8, 1945, she was liberated.

She knew the dangers of going home. She had heard that two Jewish boys had been killed and a young woman severely injured. Nonetheless she went home, searching for a birth certificate. She needed to prove her identity, to confirm to herself that she had survived. There she learned that her entire family had been killed.

A few days later she went to Chrzanów, where she was invited to stay in the friendly farmer's home. Since the house had no

---

*Erika married Joseph Burger and immigrated to Canada in 1968. They have three children and eight grandchildren.

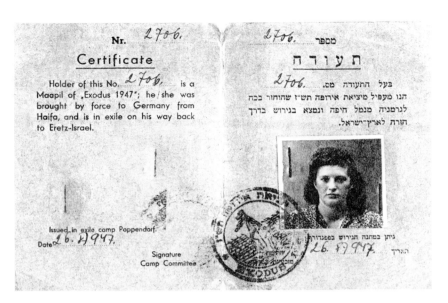

Nr. 2706.

Certificate

Holder of this No. 2706. is a Maapil of „Exodus 1947"; he / she was brought by force to Germany from Haifa, and is in exile on his way back to Eretz-Israel.

Issued in exile camp Poppendorf.
Date 26. 8 947.

Signature
Camp Committee

2706. מספר

ת ע ו ד ה

2706.

בעל התעודה מס.
הנו מעפיל מיציאת אירופה תש"ז שהוחזר בכח
לגרמניה מנמל חיפה ונמצא בגירוש בדרך
חזרת לארץ-ישראל.

ניתן במחנה הגירוש בפפנדורף
26. 8 947.   התאריך

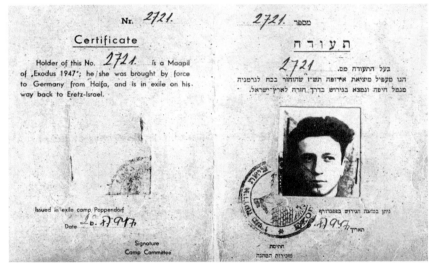

Nr. 2721.

Certificate

Holder of this No. 2721. is a Maapil of „Exodus 1947"; he / she was brought by force to Germany from Haifa, and is in exile on his way back to Eretz-Israel.

Issued in exile camp Poppendorf.
Date 26. 8 947.

Signature
Camp Committee

2721. מספר

ת ע ו ד ה

2721.

בעל התעודה מס.
הנו מעפיל מיציאת אירופה תש"ז שהוחזר בכח לגרמניה
מנמל חיפה ונמצא בגירוש בדרך. חזרה לארץ-ישראל.

חתימת
מזכירות המחנה

Identity documents for Sara Wiener and her husband, Chanina Kam, issued by the Haganah in the summer of 1947.

inside toilet, it was natural that she would go out late at night. She dug up the tin box with the gold coins and the next day left for Lublin. Of all her family's property, she abandoned everything and sold only the mill for some nearly worthless Polish zlotys. The gold coins bought her food and clothes.

In Lublin, she joined a group of thirty-five young people who formed what they called Kibbutz Lanegev and prepared to go to

Palestine. They studied farming, Jewish and Zionist history, Hebrew, and survival skills. Sara became a teacher, teaching Hebrew and the songs she remembered along with the new songs she learned from the Zionist leaders.

In June 1946, with her group of friends and their leader, she made the trek from Lublin to the French harbor town of Sète and boarded the *Exodus.*

• • •

When the Germans invaded Poland, Chanina Kam, born in 1928 in Komarow, Lublin province in Poland, fled with his family to the cities of Zlatoust and Chelyabinsk in the Ural Mountains. He knew nothing about Palestine. Zionism was a crime in Russia. He lived with his mother and two brothers, while his father served for a time in the Red Army. "The war years in the U.S.S.R. were terrible," he later wrote me. "In June 1946, we returned to Poland, but we didn't go back to our home. It was destroyed. We never tried to regain our property. We knew it was useless. Who will pay for something if he can get it for nothing?"

When he learned that twenty-three members of his family had been shot and burned, he became a Zionist. He dreamed of becoming a farmer in a kibbutz in Palestine. He joined a kibbutz group in Poland and with them trekked across Europe by foot, trucks, and trains, spending a few days in Vienna in the Rothschild Hospital DP camp, and in a former Hitler Youth Camp at Geretsried, south of Munich. "After what we suffered," he wrote, "this was like a paradise on this earth." From there he traveled to Marseille and in Sète, boarded the *Exodus,* determined to live in Palestine.*

The American boys talked with the people, and found that the Jews were on the march and nothing could stop them. They were Jews of the miracle, Jews who had climbed back onto earth out of the inferno which had trapped and burned six million, Jews who had been liberated by the GIs and the Tommies and the Red Army boys, and because of the miracle of their own

*Chanina Kam and Sara Wiener met on a kibbutz in Israel. They fell in love and married. Sara became a teacher and Chanina an electronics specialist. They have two children and two grandchildren.

The younger children move along the dock with fear. They do not know what lies ahead.

lives, they began to believe in the miracle. Maybe their wives were alive, their sons, their daughters—anyone who could link them to the past. So they took their little packs of concentration-camp clothes and marched east out of Dachau and Bergen-Belsen, out of Buchenwald and Auschwitz. They came home to Lodz and Warsaw, to Pilsen and Bratislava, to the villages and the cities in which they had been born. But their wives were dead, their sons were dead, their daughters were dead, and it seemed to them that the smell of blood was in the streets. They knew they could no longer live in the towns and the villages they had dreamed of, so they left and went west again, to Germany, to the death land, because the Americans were there and the Americans had big hearts and maybe the Americans would help them go to Palestine.

And when they began to lose faith even in the Americans, when the quotas were never open, the visas never given, and the gates forever shut, they crawled out of the degradation of the DP camps, and went down to secret ports in Italy and France, and climbed on leaky fishing boats or the *Exodus 1947*, and they ran the whole British blockade. Sometimes they escaped the British, and jumped off the ships and mingled with the Jews in Palestine, who rushed to the shore to help them land. More often, their ships were caught and they were sent to Cyprus. There they waited. In a year, maybe two years, maybe three or four years, they could get to Palestine legally, with a visa. Every month the

Some of the soldiers try to comfort the frightened children.

Staying within their age groups, more than six hundred teenagers and children gradually disembark.

British gave 750 certificates to the Jews on the prison island. Some of the American crew on other Haganah ships had mingled with the refugees at Haifa and were waiting now in Cyprus. The boys talked of them as if they were heroes.

The American boys began to identify themselves with the refugees. Bill Bernstein tried to explain in a letter to his mother why they had set out on such a voyage.

> You ask me to settle down, go to school. That's all very fine, Mom, but one doesn't find happiness by continually telling himself he's

happy. Don't you think I would like a nice wife and kids and a good job? Of course I would, but I can't do that now. I say this knowing that your thoughts and heart are with me wherever I am and whatever I'm doing. If I lose that, I lose the only things that I own.

The Americans, who had been outsiders helping, now began to feel like the refugees themselves. "The time isn't far off when we'll redeem our honor," Bill wrote in a letter to his brother. "Perhaps you and I won't be around when it happens, but I can see it building all around me. The base of the pyramid is slow in building but the pinnacle comes quickly. . . . This is it! After working, hiding, and chasing all over Europe, we are finally on our way."

The boys talked to one another soberly. "I'm going to keep going back and forth from Europe on these trips as long as I can. I want to be there when the last DP gets out of Germany."

Like few ships sailing the seven seas, the *Exodus 1947* dropped traditional barriers. All day the officers and the crew and the passengers sang songs, told stories, ate the food from America, and drank rationed water out of their refugee bottles. The crew broadcast news programs for the passengers in four languages. In the evening, the musicians among them took out their accordions and mandolins, and the people sang songs under the clear blue stars of the Mediterranean and dreamed of the land they had never seen.

The Palyam men, faced with the daunting task of caring for 4,500 people in a ship built to hold 400, divided the people into groups of twenty and thirty with their own leaders. They brought them food and water so efficiently that feeding the 4,500 people was completed in forty-five minutes. They hid the people belowdecks, from the eyes of British planes and destroyers patrolling the Mediterranean. They regulated the time the refugees could spend on the upper of the four decks for fresh air. They fixed the hours the children were bathed with hoses full of seawater. They showed the pregnant women and the mothers with small children where to hide in the bottom hold of the ship if they were attacked by the British destroyers. And they prepared the young men and women for battling with potatoes and tin cans of food.

One day, Shmuel's wife, Pola, gave birth to her child and a few hours later she died. The Americans were the honor guard. Pola lay in state for a few hours, with the flag of Zion and its Magen Dovid, the Star of David, spread over her. One of the crew read the burial service.

"We are burying today," he said, "without marker, one more Jew to be added to the list of those millions who have died in recent years. We are reminded of the first exodus, when countless numbers of Jews also were buried in nameless graves. We go again to our land. If there can be any compensation for the death of this woman, it is that we here consecrate ourselves and gain courage for those tasks which are yet ahead. The way of Aliyah Beth is a hard way. It is, we believe, the only way."

Then it happened. Before dawn, at 2:00 A.M., on Friday, July 18, the *Exodus 1947* was attacked. The ship was running east, heading for Gaza, on the southern coast of Palestine. It was about twenty miles off the coast. The destroyers shouted at the boys not to fight back or beach the ship. They said, "You are in territorial waters. Stop your ship. We are going to board you." They said it from behind big searchlights, huge blue searchlights that blinded the people. The crew shouted it wasn't true; their charts showed that they were outside territorial waters.

Two destroyers came alongside and snapped the *Exodus 1947* between them. They caught her on a wave; the people swung in the air, the *Exodus* shook as though she would sink, then she settled carefully back on the water. The noise of the yelling and of the ramming were like something out of hell.

Bill Bernstein pulled hard on the whistle cord. It sent out a bloodcurdling scream. Every light on the ship was turned on. The destroyers kept their blue spotlights on the *Exodus,* so every part of the battle could be seen. The searchlights lit up the Magen Dovids flying high.

A hundred hands on the destroyers came through the searchlights at once and tossed strings of firecrackers at the *Exodus.* The firecrackers sounded like machine-gun fire. They lit up the ship like incendiaries. A hundred more arms were raised in the searchlights and threw tear-gas bombs. The two things, the fire-crackers and the tear gas, did just what artillery does on a battle-field before a charge: they scared the *Exodus* people for a minute.

In that minute about eighteen British sailors rushed down the drawbridge of the destroyer and leaped onto the boat's deck, right outside the wheelhouse door. The British sailors wore hard leather shields around their left arms to ward off the people's blows. They were armed with pistols and clubs. The *Exodus 1947* passengers and crew were armed with potatoes and tins of kosher beef. The British sailors emptied their pistols through the closed door of the wheelhouse. Then they dashed in, swinging their clubs. They hit Bill Bernstein on the left temple. He fell uncon-scious and was carried to the captain's stateroom.

Nat Nadler, the electrician, described what happened next. "Big Bill Millman, the six-foot-four bosun, and I were on the port side of the chart room adjacent to the wheelhouse. Bill said, 'Go see where Bernstein is. He hasn't come out yet.'

"I went into the chart room. I saw Bernstein being taken care of by a few women. Two British marines appeared from the wheelhouse. I started fighting with them. They clubbed me and knocked me out. When I came to, I was bleeding profusely. I had lost my glasses. I crawled out of the chart room blinded by the tear gas. Bill was looking for me on the port side. He entered the chart room and started fighting with the two marines. He grabbed one of them by the groin and the neck and dragged him outside, hoping to throw him overboard. The other marine shot at his head. The bullet hit him in the chin. His jaw was shattered.

"I crawled back to the improvised hospital on B deck aft, and a refugee doctor sewed up the wound around my eye. I was put in a bunk and saw that Bill Millman was in a bunk above me. He had a voice you could have heard all over the ship. Now he could hardly talk, but he said, 'We really showed them, Nat. Didn't we?'

"'Yeah, we really showed 'em, you big jerk. Look at you. Your whole head is bandaged.'"

Nat went on. "I couldn't tolerate lying still while all the action was going on. I went back on deck. I saw Murray Aronoff, a deckhand from the Bronx, leading a whole bunch of refugees, running around with a fire ax, scaring the hell out of the British sailors and marines."

Nat's blue eyes were tearing. "I was furious that the British were killing people. I jumped on a marine. I pulled his helmet back. His chin strap was fastened under his neck, choking him. Two refugees and I threw him into the sea."

He stopped for a moment, then continued. "David Lowenthal from Pittsburgh released one of the life rafts, which weighed a ton, and dropped it on the deck of one of the destroyers."

His face grew soft. "Not all the marines were brutal. One of them leaped aboard, took a look at the people in front of him, pulled off his helmet, and jumped over the side."

Uri Urmacher, who had survived the slaughter of the orphan car in Poland, stood near a porthole with his friend, sixteen-year-old Hirsch Yakubovich, watching the sailors and marines climb on the deck. Hirsch, an orphan who had come from the DP camp at Kloster-Indersdorf, was framed behind the slats of a big life raft. He tossed an orange at a marine. The marine shot him in the face and killed him.

Mordecai Baumstein, another orphan, who had come from the DP camp at Bad Reichenhall, was fighting with fruit and canned food when a marine shot him in the stomach. He was the third to die.

Little Bracha, who dreamed of the land of oranges, terrified by the ramming of the ship, was sure she was going to die. Even her mother's promise that they were nearing that land of oranges could not console her.

The ramming, the tear gas burning their eyes and choking them, made some of the younger children hysterical. The leaders, their eyes burning also, tried to keep the groups together.

The boys of sixteen and seventeen, most of them orphans from DP camps, were real fighters. They kept beating off the British, with nothing for armament but their grocery store of potatoes and canned food, a few steam jets, and sticks chopped from the banisters. They stayed up on the hurricane deck and the boat deck, while the women and babies were kept belowdecks.

The destroyers kept ramming the *Exodus*, trying to land boarding parties. The people threw some of their life rafts down, to prevent the sailors from coming aboard. They captured all the sailors except the six in the wheelhouse, where Bill lay dying. They locked the captured sailors in staterooms. The British sailors in the wheelhouse were prisoners too, but they controlled the rudder. They were steering a straight course for Haifa. The boys tried to retake the wheelhouse and failed. The British sailors were armed.

Ike and Cy Weinstein made their way through the passengers, many of whom were terrified and weeping, and went down to the steering engine. They disconnected the cable leading to the wheel, and the ship was under the command of the American crew again. The crew started to zigzag; that made it impossible for the British to land any more boarding parties. The destroyers rammed them, this time not to land more men, but to disable them. They rammed the *Exodus* amidships, trying to foul the steering gear. The only thing that kept the British from cutting the *Exodus* in half was the heavy fender that steamers in America use for protection against pilings. The 4,500 refugees from Europe were saved because American steamers are built with fenders.

During the battle, John Stanley Grauel, the student-preacher, invited several British sailors to his cabin, fed them his best liquor, surreptitiously locked the door of the cabin, and effectively kept them out of the battle. In a confidential report to London written a few days after the battle, Lieutenant R.J.G. MacPherson, of the destroyer HMS *Chieftain*, warned the British navy:

> It is submitted that Boarding Parties may be most strongly warned of the danger of familiarity with the American Jew-runners, and especially against accepting offers of alcoholic refreshment. They are extremely pliable fellows after they have ceased opposition, and it is easy to forget that they are criminals with a decided pecuniary interest in regaining control of the vessel if they see any chance of doing it.

Aboard the ship, Ike and Cy were convinced that, since they controlled the steering gear, they could bring the *Exodus* into Haifa. The little steamer, with its flat bottom, could do what no destroyer could do, it could land in the shallow waters of Haifa Bay. But Bernie Marks, the most skilled seaman of the American crew, disagreed. "I accosted Ike and Yossi Harel with the intention of reminding them that we were responsible for forty-five hundred innocent souls. It seemed to me that they were ready to accept the fact that we were not going to break through that huge armada surrounding us." When Dr. Cohen told the commander, Yossi Harel, that at least five people or more would die if they did not have immediate blood transfusions, Yossi and Bernie decided the lives of the wounded refugees and crew were more important than a symbolic victory at sea. Ike then joined the two men. "We held a short conference on the boat deck," Bernie told me, "and we three agreed to surrender. I was to act as captain for two reasons: one, to protect Ike because he was an Israeli and it would go hard for him if he were captured; and two, to bring this act of piracy before the World Court in the Hague. But the Israelis decided not to pursue this case, though I was willing, and I immediately went back to being first mate."

Through the loudspeaker Yossi announced to the people that the *Exodus* was surrendering. He asked the British to please send up doctors and medicines for the wounded. The atmosphere changed immediately. The British medics showed genuine concern. Dr. D.C.S. Betts, the surgeon lieutenant of the Royal Navy who boarded the *Exodus* from the destroyer HMS *Chequers*, later reported to London:

> All our sailors, having used force very successfully to establish control, were extremely helpful in tending the wounded. I know of one who became involved in a slight skirmish after I came aboard, and knocked his opponent down and rendered him useless for further combat, and then proceeded immediately to administer first aid from the pack he was carrying. I have great admiration for all of them.

At about four in the afternoon, the *Exodus* came slowly into Haifa Harbor. Grauel, who came ashore, was arrested by the British, his papers were taken away, and he was then released. "I accuse the British," he told us. "I accuse the British of attacking us outside of territorial waters. I accuse the British of attacking an unarmed vessel on the high seas. I accuse the British of an act of piracy."

The British version of the boarding, in which they indirectly answered the charges of piracy, differed from John Grauel's. Referring to the *Exodus* by its former name, the *President Warfield*, the official government communiqué, issued July 19, 1947, read:

In order to remove any doubts which may have been raised by inaccurate broadcasts from the illegal immigrant ship *President Warfield*, the following facts are recorded:—

The *President Warfield* arrived in Palestinian waters early on the 18th of July, carrying approximately 5,000 Jewish illegals. In order to avoid being boarded she took violent evasive action which in the ensuing boarding operation resulted in damage to herself as well as to ships of the Royal Navy. Her sides had been planked up and barbed wire had been strung fore and aft. The boarding party met strong resistance backed up by tear smoke, fire-works, smoke bombs, steam jets and various missiles. She also dropped life rafts from a height on to the decks of the naval vessels.

One single shot, and one burst of machine-gun fire were used by one of the naval ships against an immigrant who was threatening to decapitate one of the boarding party with an axe, and another who was about to use a rifle. The shot and burst missed, but frightened the men who dropped their weapons. No other fire was used by naval personnel. Some fifty naval personnel in all were used in the boarding party.

The *President Warfield* entered Haifa Port under her own steam on the evening of the 18th. Two illegal immigrants were found to have died from fractured skulls, and a third has since died in the hospital from the same cause. Twenty-seven others were admitted to Haifa Hospital; some of these persons, though not all, were suffering from injuries received when the *President Warfield* was boarded. Three naval ratings were injured and admitted to hospital.

The eleven members of the United Nations Special Committee on Palestine (UNSCOP) were in Jerusalem when the Swedish chairman of the committee, Justice Emil Sandstrom, and Vladimir Simic, the Yugoslav delegate, drove to Haifa to see the operation. Sandstrom, shocked by the sight of the wounded ship and the British soldiers leading bandaged people to the three so-called hospital ships, said, "Britain must no longer have the mandate over Palestine."*

For days nobody connected in any way with the *Exodus 1947* could sleep. A group of American sailors who had come off other illegal Haganah ships came to see me, to hear whatever I could tell them about the *Exodus* and its American crew and to reminisce about their own experiences. They were handsome boys. There was a tall dark boy whose Brooklyn accent even I, a native, found extraordinary. He spoke quickly, as though he were chewing bubble gum and blowing each sentence into a balloon. There was a boy from Atlanta, with a soft, slurring accent that seemed far from home in the tense port of Haifa. There was a young student from Harvard who looked barely seventeen, who was following the scientific footsteps of Chaim Weizmann. They were by no means all Zionists, but they had all determined to do something to help the Jews.

They paced up and down, smoking cigarettes to hide their emotions, plucking at grapes on the coffee table, reminiscing about their own ships like men reminiscing about a great leader at a wake.

We could look down at the Mediterranean, twinkling with lights, and at the skeletons of dead illegal ships. The British war-

*Back in New York, UNSCOP recommended to the General Assembly that the United Nations create a Jewish state. The UN then voted to partition Palestine into a Jewish state and an Arab state. The Arabs walked out of the UN and declared war against the Jews.

ships were back in the harbor. The boys from Brooklyn and Atlanta, from earlier Haganah ships, told me how they had decided
to mingle with the refugees when their ships were captured by
the British and go as DPs to Cyprus. "For us, Cyprus was a new
hell altogether," a boy from the *Hatikvah* told me. "For the
refugees, Cyprus was just hell with a new flag. For a month we
didn't sleep in a bed. For a month we lived on Spam and a little
gray bread and some colored water called tea. For a month we
lived without water. We never knew in America what it meant to
live without water. We didn't know how a man loses his dignity
and his self-respect when he has no water. We stole water from
each other. We rushed from one compound and one tin hut to
another to search for water all day."

The boys smoked more cigarettes. They paced more nervously. They seemed to hate themselves again, remembering.
But they marveled at the refugees. "There they were on Cyprus,
in a camp with two walls of barbed wire, but still the refugees
shaved each day with salt water. Still they washed each day with a
thimbleful of water, left in the slop after all the water had been
used up for cooking. They kept their dignity.

"There was nothing to do all day. You couldn't read, you
couldn't write, you couldn't study; you couldn't even practice
Hebrew"—that strange romantic language that had been picked
up from the dead and turned into a language for a vital living
people. "You couldn't even think. It was too hot on Cyprus. And
there was no water."

The American sailors grew bitter. They wondered if it was
worth all the trouble. They wondered why they had ever left
Boston and Brooklyn, Harvard and UCLA and their good busi-
nesses, to sit and rot in hell. The American sailors picked up scabies. And still there was no water, and no sanitation. Their
scabies became infected. They couldn't sit or lie down or sleep.
They were comfortable only when they stood. And they felt like
Job himself.

Then there were nine certificates available for Palestine. Nine
Americans from one illegal Haganah ship had all planned to go

together and then return to Europe as a solid crew on another ship. But now they insisted that the three sickest sailors go first, and that the other six certificates be given to pregnant women whose babies could then be born in Palestine. The other sailors would wait. It might be two more years in hell. They would wait.

The three sick sailors stood in line with the refugees in the hot Cyprus sun from six in the morning until ten, queuing up just to turn back to the prison guards the tins from which they had eaten. The British made sure the refugees were taking nothing with them from the Crown Colony of Cyprus, none of the shirts and dresses the women had made out of pieces of their tents to cover their nakedness.

They were screened five or six times before they could leave for Palestine. At six in the evening, without having eaten or drunk all day, they were put on board a prison ship, behind the squirrellike prison cage. Women and babies, men and young people, all were pushed down the steep stairs to the hold. There were no beds, no chairs, no blankets. The floors were filthy with food from the last voyage. Those who had brought blankets with them from Europe to Cyprus, and from Cyprus to Palestine, spread their blankets and slept. Those who had brought no blankets with them slept on the floor.

The American sailors from the Haganah ships that had come before the *Exodus 1947* were sick with their own bitterness. The sailors from Brooklyn and Harvard and Atlanta had good homes to go back to. They could just get up and go back and talk about all of this as the great adventure of their lives. It was summer now, and they could talk about these six months of their exodus for years to come, until the whole adventure had boiled itself down to one or two pictures. But for the refugees, this was no adventure. This was the end of unreality. This was the place they had dreamed of in the concentration camps, the place they had fought to reach in the DP camps, the place they had sweated for in Cyprus: the goal.

And remembering the people as their faces lit up in the morning, seeing the cliff dwellings on Mount Carmel, the American sailors decided that it had not been in vain. The sailor from Atlanta looked down at the graveyard where his ship lay rotting in the Mediterranean. "I'm going to stay here awhile and learn the language and see the people and how they live. Then I'm going back to Europe to bring another shipload over."

Indeed, soon after, I learned that a ship called the *Shivat Zion*, carrying refugees from Morocco and Algeria, had been captured by the British sailors and was moored at the Haifa wharf.

The next morning we began to ferret out what had happened to the crew of the *Exodus 1947*. The Jews of Palestine were obviously spending long hours in the Tel Aviv theaters studying Hollywood movies. With a technique that combined the best in Superman and Edward G. Robinson, Ike, Yossi, and some of the other Palmach and Palyam members hid in secret caches on the *Exodus*, waiting until the dock was cleared. They slipped through the whole barrage of barbed wire, tanks, trucks, MPs, CID men, and Major Cardozo's army of gunners. They were walking calmly now through the hot streets of Haifa, hiding behind nothing except sunglasses.

During the battle at sea, many of the crew had been exposed as Americans. But the British navy and the British army were apparently not on intimate speaking terms. The navy merely captured the boys; it was the army's job to imprison them. The navy walked off the battered *Exodus* at Haifa, said good-bye to some of the boys whose liquor they helped finish, and even chuckled when some of the Americans said, "So long. Be seeing you again soon."

Most of the boys, like brawny Dov Miller from Brooklyn, ruffled the hair on their naked chests a little more, pretended during the interrogation on the dock that they spoke no English, and were now scattered on the prison ships headed, presumably, for Cyprus.

The British had to make some arrests. They arrested Bernie Marks and Cy Weinstein and put them into the police lockup on the dock. I learned that Cy Weinstein was the first one thrown into jail.

"It looked—well—the whole thing was just like a storybook," he told me. "The big concrete door with a little grilled window;

A few days after the Exodus *lands, the* Shivat Zion, *a small ship from North Africa, arrives in Haifa with Moroccan and Algerian refugees.*

An Orthodox Moroccan and his shy daughter are gently prodded along the wharf as they learn they are going to Cyprus.

dirty cell, cement floor, no furniture, no cot, just a filthy roll covered with cockroaches and the only light came from a little grilled window high up in the wall. I kept thinking of that movie—you know, *The Lives of a Bengal Lancer*. The first thing I did was to see what chances I had to escape. I began to scale the wall, and finally got up so I could look out. All I could see was a big stone wall with an Arab policeman, carrying a machine gun and walking back and forth. I jumped down, and sat on the floor and tried to think. Some Arab policemen kept walking back and forth in the corridor, and each time, they'd peek in the little grilled window to take a look at me.

"Then I heard some noises in the corridor. And I heard Marks's voice. 'Hey, Bernie,' I yelled, 'I'm in here.'

The North African refugees have printed a sarcastic thanks to the British for capturing and battling them at sea.

The last reluctant refugees are dragged off the embattled Shivat Zion *by steel-helmeted British soldiers.*

" 'Take it easy,' one of the Limeys said. 'He'll be along after a while. We're interrogating him first.'

"Bernie came in. We had a bull session going over the whole thing, telling each other what happened. Each of us had seen a different part of the battle.

"We figured out how we could escape. The hinges on the door were inside the room. We could unscrew them, overpower the guard, get the ammunition which was in a room across the corridor, jump off the dock, and swim away. But we never did it. We sometimes thought we'd do it just for fun. Unscrew the hinges and when the guard unlocked the door, he'd fall on his face.

"The British had all our clothes. They took everything we owned. We came off without shoes, just with what we could find. I found my long underwear and my box of pastels. I took the pastels and painted a big flag of Zion across the whole cell wall. Ritzer took red crayon and printed under it WE'VE JUST BEGUN TO FIGHT.

"The Limey guard saw it and yelled through the grilled window, 'I'm bringing you a pail of water to wash that wall right away. We keep these cells clean.'

" 'Water,' I said. 'Oh brother, what I could do with water. My feet are filthy. They're just longing for water.' "

The boys were kept in the lockup for two days. While they were lying in their own filth, unshaven, wearing only their dirty shorts from the battle, the door opened. Bernie Marks was taken to a room in the front of the jail. A high-ranking Bristish naval officer named Morgan, wearing immaculate white trousers and a screaming white shirt, wanted to talk to him. "He first inquired if I was a sailor," Bernie told me, "and I said 'Yes sir.' Then he said, 'Don't you know how dangerous this business is?' I answered, 'Yes, it is very dangerous—but after Hitler, these people will not live anywhere but Palestine, and no matter what you throw at them, they will keep coming.'"

Morgan continued, "I commanded one of the ships that engaged you in battle."

Bernie launched right into an offensive. "Why did you ram us outside territorial waters?"

"I didn't come here to talk politics," Morgan said. "I came here to talk sailor to sailor."

Bernie stood up with dignity. "Yes?"

"I just wanted to tell you that your ship could have been sunk. That's all."

Bill Bernstein never regained consciousness. He died of the blow on the head he received during the fight in the wheelhouse. His body was wrapped in an American flag, to be buried in Martyrs' Row in Haifa Cemetery. The three boys were let out of jail to become Bill's pallbearers. They were still in their dirty clothes from the ship. They had washed, but they hadn't shaved. They were put in a truck. They sat beside Bill's body, which was sealed in a coffin, and beside the bodies of Hirsch Yakubovich and Mordecai Baumstein, who were just wrapped in simple shrouds, two DPs who had lived just long enough to be buried in Palestine.

The bodies had already begun to smell. It was a hot summer day. The American boys walked through the cemetery carrying the coffin.

"I was awfully confused," Cy told me. "Bill, Bill, Bill—I was carrying Bill's body—in Palestine. It didn't make sense."

Back on the *Exodus 1947*, Bill had had the feeling that it would happen to him.

3

Cyprus

EVERYTHING POINTED TO IT—the *Exodus 1947* people were to go to Cyprus; the baggage labels, the mimeographed notes the British sailors had passed around on the ship, Major Cardozo's reassurance that the families separated in the search tents would be reunited in the prison camp.

Everything pointed to it, but when the prison ships left Haifa, they disappeared. The British army had prepared the dock in Famagusta for the ships, and they did not come. Inside the camps in Cyprus, the prisoners cleared space on the floors of their tents to welcome the newcomers. Some hurried to the barbed-wire barricades and stood waiting in the heat to catch the first glimpse of the new arrivals. Maybe their relatives were among the *Exodus* people. But a day of waiting stretched to three and longer. And in London there was a total blackout of news.

I decided to fly to Cyprus. The British had consistently barred correspondents from entering the prison camps. They made no difficulties for me, though I was the only correspondent attached to the United Nations Special Committee on Palestine to whom they gave a visa. In two hours, I flew the two hundred miles from Tel Aviv's Lydda Airport to Cyprus. My headquarters were the Savoy Hotel in Famagusta, the port city where Morris Laub and

I fly to Cyprus to wait for the three "hospital ships." No correspondents are allowed in the camp. I am smuggled in by Joshua Leibner, the assistant director of the Joint Distribution Committee as a new member of his staff. On my first day in the camp, I talk with the refugees from earlier ships. They tell me they have come to the barricades hoping they will see the arrival of the Jews of the Exodus. Maybe their mother has come, their father, their wife, their child, perhaps a friend—anyone who can bring them news of their loved ones.

the director of the JDC, the American Jewish Joint Distribution Committee, welcomed me.

With them or with some British officers, I drove each day to the two camps in which the British detained the Jews: Caraolos, on the edge of the tiny harbor of Famagusta, and Xylotimbu, thirty miles away. The *Exodus* people were to be housed at a third campsite, just being cleared.

You had to smell Cyprus to believe it. You had to smell the latrines for twenty thousand people to believe it—and you didn't

It is a shock to see the grim architecture of the death camps reborn in Cyprus—the ubiquitous watchtower, the long dirt road walled in on both sides by concentration camp poles and barbed wire.

The barren tin huts and death camp poles stretch to the horizon.

believe it. You had to smell the sweat of men and women as they cooked the food over open stoves and the sweat poured into their pots and pans; you had to smell the garbage which piled up waiting for the trucks which didn't come to believe it—and you didn't believe it. Each evening I left the prison camps and went back to the Savoy Hotel and showered for an hour, but I felt I could never wash the smell away.

You had to smell Cyprus to believe it.

Here the Jews, whose only crime is that they tried to go to Palestine, live without water, without plumbing, without lights, without privacy, blistering in summer heat, freezing in the wet frost of the Cypriot winters.

Twice a day, a small British truck drives through the camps carrying water.

A young husband and wife, standing outside their tent, are ecstatic. They have water.

The American boys had described it well. Cyprus was a twentieth-century purgatory, a hot hell of desert sand and wind blowing against tents and tin Nissen huts, a hell circumscribed by two walls of barbed wire whose architecture had come out of Dachau and Treblinka, a hell in which privacy was unknown.

There was no water in Cyprus. All day, some twenty thousand adults and two thousand orphaned children stood at the barbed wire and looked out at the Mediterranean which creamed their shore, but they had no water. Each day a few small boys stood in

The people swarm around the truck carrying anything that will hold water: a tin cup, an empty can, a bucket.

the midday heat, clutching the gate with their hands, their eyes fixed on the road outside the barbed-wire boundary of the camp. Behind them, down the long rows of silent nameless streets, the population retreated into the thin shadows of tents and Nissen huts, trying to escape the burning assault of the sun.

The boys' ears caught the sound of a motor. They waited until the squat British water truck materialized out of the dust. Then they flew down the camp street shouting "*Wasser! Wasser!*" Other small boys sprang out of the stillness and took up the cry. "*Voda!*" "*L'eau!*" "*Agua!*" "*Veez!*" A man ran out of a tent carrying a five-gallon tin. A woman followed him with an evaporated-milk can. Everyone dropped the nothing he was doing, grabbed anything that would hold water, and rushed to the truck. The latecomers from the last illegal ships carried only cups. They hesitated on the fringe of the crowd. They would soon learn to scrounge or steal bigger tins like the five-gallon one the first man had, and fight their way to the head of the queue without ceremony.

People pushed and shoved and clawed in a festering commotion to get to the spigots. A red-faced girl jostled a bearded old man and upset his basin. The old man watched the hot ground drink up his ration. A man slapped an urchin's wrists and the boy threw half a cupful of water extravagantly in his face. A youth shinnied up onto the tank and pounded it madly, as if he expected a spring to spurt from under his hand. The tank emptied quickly and the people moved carefully away with their treasure. The driver, a blond British corporal who had been standing silently by with his arms folded, climbed back into his cab and drove away, with the tank spilling silver droplets onto the burning gravel road.

Back in a hut, an old woman sipped a little water from a cup. Under a tent fly a young man named Moshe—it was he who had carried the five-gallon tin—began to shave, wetting his razor in a saucer. His wife, Tova, stretched a brassiere and a faded pair of shorts on a board. She sprinkled water on them with a teaspoon and attacked them with a chunk of yellow soap. She worked slowly because of the heat and because she was heavily pregnant.

With infinite pains she sprinkled the garments again with the spoon, rubbed another spot with soap, poured another teaspoon of water, and after an hour, she had a fresh brassiere and clean shorts with which to face the desert community.

Moshe had used up all the water in the saucer; he wiped his razor and put it away. The old woman lay down on a palm mat and fanned herself listlessly with a dirty handkerchief, pausing now and then to mop the sweat off her face. A humid, humming silence moved through the alleys and streets again as the Caraolos camp gave up to the heat and slipped back into the long coma of waiting.

A youngster pounds on the empty water tank, hoping he can retrieve a few drops. The British driver, a corporal, disinterested in the boy, asks me to take his photo.

They defy the prison camp—

This was the Crown Colony of Cyprus, in the eastern Mediterranean. The travel books called it "romantic Cyprus." The Greeks called it "love's island," because Aphrodite was born of foam off its shores. Here Richard the Lionhearted was married and Othello wooed Desdemona. Here now the Jews, whose crime was that they wanted to go to Palestine, lived in confinement without plumbing or electricity, blistering in the summer sun, shivering in winter's miserable wetness. Here now we waited for 4,500 more Jews from the *Exodus* to be imprisoned.

The British had established these internment camps in 1946 to stop the Jews fleeing from the DP camps of Germany on the underground route to Palestine. "Perhaps," a British officer had said, "if the illegal Jewish immigrants realize that they are going to wind up here, they may not be so anxious to crowd aboard their stinking hellships and try to get to Palestine."

Instead the traffic steadily increased. The caïque *Palmach*, named after the striking force of the Haganah, came from Italy and Greece with 630 people. The *Knesseth Israel* followed with 3,900. In the spring of 1947 the *Theodor Herzl* brought 2,640 more. In twelve months some twenty-five thousand Jews on twenty-three ships were captured and diverted to Cyprus. Caraolos, the first camp, was bursting. It was a collection of five separate compounds, including one for orphans. Now it held 6,000 refugees. Xylotimbu was opened before the barest necessities could be provided. It was already overflowing with 11,000 Holocaust survivors. Finally the British permitted 750 Jews each month to transfer to Palestine.

So Cyprus became another station, a kind of suburb, for the strange modern exodus of the children of Israel out of the wilderness of postwar Europe to the so-long-promised Promised Land.

—and survive.

The lucky ones leave the camps legally for Palestine. Each month 750 refugees in Cyprus and 750 in the DP camps in Europe are given certificates for the Holy Land. It is the quota the British set up in 1939 when they planned to end all Jewish immigration to Palestine in five years.

Each day we waited in this suburb of sorrow for news of the *Exodus*, but in place of news, rumors began to spiral through the camp. *"They're not bringing the* Exodus *people here!" "They're taking them to a camp in Eritrea." "A new camp is being built for them in Tobruk." "They're taking them to Germany." "No, no, not Germany!"*

Days went by. I found myself hoping that maybe the *Exodus* people wouldn't come here. For in the inescapable intimacy of the camp, human dignity had begun to decay. Moshe told me of the time he had intruded into a tent, looking for a friend. Four women were sitting on the floor, trying to sew. In a far corner, behind the stifling and impromptu privacy of an army blanket, a man and a wife were seeking love in the only way Cyprus afforded them. The women did not speak, but with their eyes

The order of departure is first in, first out. There are exceptions for the sick, for whom the healthier prisoners give up their certificates and continue waiting.

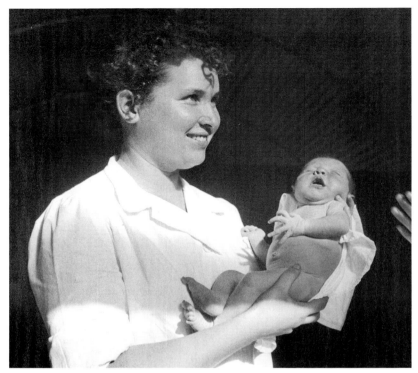

A nurse midwife holds up the newborn she has just delivered in the prison wing of the British Military Hospital in Nicosia. She tells me, "Every woman here wants a child."

"We love life," the young mother says. "That's why we want to bring new lives into the world."

they said, *We do not watch; but there is no place else for us to go.* And in Xylotimbu one day a girl had asked Josh Leibner of the JDC if she could use his kitchen shack that night. "I am getting married this afternoon," she said, "and I'd like to use it for our honeymoon. It is the only place we can be alone."

In the next days I began to hope, unrealistically, that maybe the British government, being a Labour government, would relent and allow these people to enter Palestine.

They tell me, "This is our answer to Hitler: 'You can have a child and live.'"

The life juices that dried up
in the death camps return in
Cyprus. Seven hundred and
fifty babies are born the first
year. Although born in these
stifling camps, the babies
survive.

A proud father builds a
bassinet for his child out of
scraps of material he finds on
Cyprus.

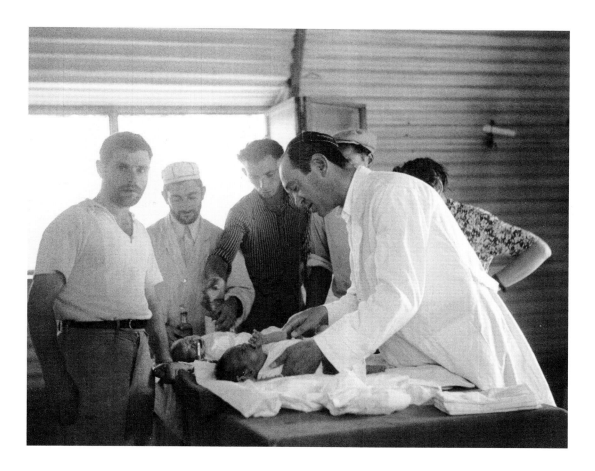

Meanwhile, life went on. In the first year on Cyprus seven hundred and fifty babies were born, and eight hundred weddings took place. I asked one of the pregnant women one day how she could bring a child into the degradation of this prison.

"Don't you know," she said to me, "don't you know that under Hitler, as soon as a Jewish woman was pregnant, she was burned? Women were the propagators of the race and they were the ones who had to be burned first. Today every woman who can have a child is determined to have one. This is our answer to Hitler. This is how we keep Israel alive. This is democracy, that you can have a child and live."

The children were born in the Jewish ward at the military hospital in Nicosia, without sheets, on blankets that were rarely changed. After a day or two they came back to the prison, their

Days are passing. The three "hospital ships" have disappeared off the face of the earth. Meanwhile, the rituals of life continue. Two baby boys are circumcised in the prison wing of the hospital while their fathers look on. One father sings the Hebrew song "Am Israel Chai": "The people of Israel live."

Little girls wear the dresses and shoes collected in Palestine and the U.S. The Joint Distribution Committee puts flesh and clothing on the bodies of the survivors.

bodies covered with rashes. But the babies survived. And the tall, kind-faced pediatrician from the Hadassah Hospital in Jerusalem, Dr. Walter Falk, told me, "Until I came here four weeks ago, I believed in science. Today I believe only in miracles."

Flies ate their bodies, but the babies survived. Their barefoot mothers, torn and ragged from the exodus and the pilgrimage, had little milk in their sagging, unwashed breasts, but the babies defied every law of bacteriology and survived.

The American Jewish JDC sent them milk and clothes and fruit and books, to supplement the army rations which the British gave them. "We're not starved here," an old man told me. "But we're prisoners behind barbed wire. We have no identity. Even the DP camps gave us a vestige of freedom and privacy and an UNRRA card with a name on it. Here even the streets are nameless, for nameless people." Yet they survived.

"Why do they keep coming, then?" Major Alexander Maitland, called "the good major" by the refugees, asked me in bewilderment. "Why can't they be patient and wait in Germany?" He knew he might as well have asked why a salmon would dash itself to pieces in a river's rapids trying to get upstream at spawning time.

"Are you British any better than our Nazi jailers?" a refugee had screamed at him hatefully one day. The next Sunday, his day off, Major Maitland spent the whole time driving up and down Cyprus searching for shoes to buy for the children of his camp.

The grimmest joke in Cyprus was a high, wooden covered bridge which the British had built for the Jews over two barbed-wire barricades in Xylotimbu, so that they could pass from one section of the camp to the other. This quickly became the refugees' Forty-second Street, and the pedestrian traffic was

The miracle of childhood. The children pose happily for the camera, while their parents climb up and down the overpass in the frustrating search for water.

A lonely child sits on a makeshift bench outside her tin hut. Her mother leans against the doorway in exhaustion. She has finished her laundry and used up most of her water.

The children ask me, "When are we going to leave? When are we going to Eretz Israel—the Land of Israel?" "I pray it will be soon," I say.

120 •

endless. As soon as a rumor spread that water was being brought to one part of the camp, or that newcomers had arrived, the people ran up and down the overpass to see if the rumor was true. The Jews ironically called the bridge the Warsaw Ghetto Bridge. In Warsaw, the Nazis too had built a bridge, to prevent the Jews from walking on Aryan streets.

They were prisoners whose horizon was sliced on four sides by vertical poles strung with pointed wire, yet they made a life for themselves inside hell. They made a creative life for themselves. They painted and drew and sewed clothes out of tent cloth; they made chess sets out of stone; they set up little industries. They had lemonade shops, shoe-repair shops, tailor shops, carpentry shops. They even made toys for their children. They tried to heal their memories by reproducing the death camps on Cypriot stone. They held exhibitions of their paintings and their carvings and the work was good enough for an art gallery in New York. Their lives were circumscribed and their horizons were the tops of tents and concentration-camp poles, but they defied the camps and survived.

The children went to school from six in the morning until twelve, when it was almost too hot to survive, and you saw sixteen-year-old boys and girls sitting in a classroom—a room built of the space between two Nissen huts with some potato sacking sewn together for a roof and some planks nailed together for a table and a bench—sixteen-year-old boys and girls going to school for the first time, learning that one plus one equals two.

They looked like no other schoolchildren in the world. There was a hunger for learning, and beneath the hunger a deep apathy and bitterness. One and one equals two. They were almost ripe for marriage and children of their own. One and one equals two.

They wore a kind of Cyprus prison uniform, a blouse and shorts, the girls almost all in faded blue, the boys in faded khaki. They didn't smile as you entered; they didn't greet you; they just sat staring. So another free person from earth had come down to hell to see what purgatory looked like. One and one equals two.

The overpass is called ironically the "Warsaw Ghetto Bridge." In wartime Warsaw, the Germans had built such bridges to keep the Jews from walking on Aryan streets. In Cyprus the bridge was built to connect different segments of the vast prison grounds. A woman in Philadelphia, seeing this image in an exhibition, screamed, "That third woman on the stairs is my mother! The man in the doorway is my father!"

The people climb the steps searching for rumors of water or news of newcomers.

What could they make of their lives? Could they pick up skills and professions? Could they be reclaimed? Could a child who had never been inside a house, who had never seen a bathtub or a flush toilet, who had long forgotten what his parents looked like before they were burned, ever be normal? One and one equals two.

They walked down the tent streets, waiting for news of the *Exodus 1947*, throwing away the rumors, and someone who had learned patience told you, "In Palestine there are olive trees and even when there is nothing on them but old bark, they go on living. Remember that." They remembered. One and one equals two.

While we waited at the dock for the ships to arrive from Haifa, I sent cables and photographs to the *Herald Tribune*. Later, the publisher, Mrs. Ogden Reid, made a secret trip to meet with Foreign Secretary Bevin at the British embassy. In her home in Manhattan, she described the meeting to me.

The ghosts of Auschwitz.
Using Cypriot stone, an
artist carves a wall hanging of a Nazi officer with
a gun in his hand and a
bandolier of ammunition
around his shoulder.
He is forcing an almost
endless line of refugees
toward the gas chamber.

They wait and go on living. They make toys for
their children.

Through their art, they begin to heal.

"I asked Bevin how they could keep thousands of Jews imprisoned in Cyprus," Mrs. Reid told me. "They've suffered enough," she told him. "They ought to be allowed to go home."

Bevin assured her that he was honored by her visit, but he could not permit more than the quota of 1,500 a month to enter Palestine—750 from Cyprus and 750 from the DP camps in Europe. The quota had been set, he told her, by the White Paper.

Bluntly, Mrs. Reid pointed out to him that the White Paper was a unilateral British document recognized only by one other country in the world—Pakistan. Bevin shifted ground; he didn't

They build an art gallery on the sand.

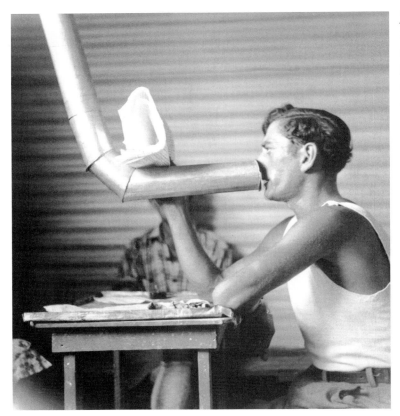

*Journalism, Cyprus style:
a newscaster broadcasts the
daily news and alerts the
people when a new ship
of refugees docks in the
Famagusta harbor.*

*They use a makeshift
iron on a makeshift
ironing board.*

They learn new skills.

think Palestine could absorb all the DPs. He regretted he could do nothing. Undaunted, Mrs. Reid and the *Herald Tribune* continued to tell the truth about the prison camps in Cyprus. What did it mean to be a Jew living in Cyprus?

It meant standing behind barbed wire for months, years perhaps. It meant that they had survived the death camps and the death marches, the DP camps, the tiny fishing boats, the illegal journey, and the British destroyers. It meant that they had put one foot on Haifa and the other foot on a prison ship to come here—to Cyprus. These were pioneers, I thought, such as the world has never known. These were people who must have the most tremendous faith or the most abject despair to come, knowing every minute and every foot of the way that the road leads through Cyprus. These are either mad people or a people with a dream that cannot be killed.

ועד הרבנים
דגולי קפריסין

Education is all-important. They are still the People of the Book.

History books, I thought, will someday write of these people as the greatest horde willingly to leave Europe, knowing that some would die and some would be killed, knowing their ships might be crushed by the British navy, knowing they would be imprisoned in this purgatory of Cyprus, yet pushing on.

One day the British made an announcement. Five hundred orphaned children were to go to Palestine at once. Other refugees, scheduled to leave, would give up their visas. The children asked that an old Hungarian violinist who had played them to sleep every night, by going from one orphan hut to another, be allowed to go with them. "He is our father," they said. The British wisely said yes.

It was Major Maitland who had hunted the shoes who broke the news to the children. He called them all together and solemnly read them the wonderful announcement in a tense voice. Their faces were utterly blank. Suddenly he understood. They knew no English. He dropped the announcement on the sand. "Look." He waved his hands. "Ship!" He fashioned a ship in the air. "Go!" He pointed outside the fence to the sea. "Palestine!" The children shrieked with joy. They jumped over the major. A little girl shyly kissed him.

Parties of farewell and rejoicing were held. People gave the youngsters precious little gifts, a photograph, a small candlestick, a doily rescued from a death camp, so that they would have happy memories of Cyprus. In the excitement nobody slept. At last, at four o'clock one morning, the time came to leave. The children returned their army blankets, their tin cups and plates. They stood in a queue and clambered aboard trucks which carried them to Famagusta. There were three prison ships. The first one, the *Empire Lifeguard*, had already sailed. The children and other adults were taken aboard the remaining two transports, the *Empire Rest* and the *Empire Comfort*. The major was at the dock. "Good-bye, Major," the children sang back at him in their few words of hastily coached English. "You are good, Major." He waved and looked away.

As the children climbed the gangway, they sang "Hatikvah." They were moving from the last suburbs of the exodus into the heart of Palestine. The ships rang with shouts and singing. They remained at anchor long after sunrise, but nobody paid any attention. There were always delays. But noon came, and three o'clock, and still the vessels had not up-anchored. It was whispered they would sail at sunset. Darkness fell and they stayed there.

"What's wrong?" somebody shouted. "Why don't we go?" The guards said nothing. Two little boys sitting on a steel staircase began to whimper.

Late in the evening, an officer appeared. "The *Empire Life-guard*," he said, "has been sabotaged in Haifa this morning. No more ships can enter this month."*

The children were led down the gangway again. On the wharf, the soldiers went through their baggage, looking for bombs. They tore up some of the gifts the people had given them so that they would have happy memories of Cyprus. There was a picture of her mother that a little girl had rescued from Auschwitz. One of the soldiers tore it into pieces. The little girl put the pieces in her palm and walked up and down the wharf, saying to everyone, "Can you help me put my mother together?"

A tired guard snatched the violin from the Hungarian violinist and broke it, looking for a bomb. The violinist knelt and gathered up the splinters of his violin and then climbed mechanically onto a truck with the rest.

It was nearly midnight now. At the camp gates there was food. Nobody touched it. The children walked silently to the gates and sat down outside the camp, refusing to enter, exhausted by the heat, by the waiting, by the confusion and the disillusionment.

They were like people who had been to the electric chair once and had escaped death and now were coming back to the chair again. A young girl inside the barbed-wire gates, watching them walk in silence, dragging their feet, observed, "That's the way they walked to the gas chambers. They never screamed. They just walked silently, like dead people."

*The sabotage was the work of the Haganah. It was an attempt to end the British quota system. The bomb exploded after everyone was off the ship. No lives were lost.

4

Port-de-Bouc

AT LAST THE NEWS came. Through their own means of getting information, the prisoners of Cyprus learned that the *Exodus* Jews were not coming. Even Cyprus was too good for them. The *Exodus* people were being returned to Port-de-Bouc in southern France. Such a move, London thought, would crush Aliyah Beth and end the illegal immigration forever. No more Jews would dare run the British blockade.

I flew back to Jerusalem, rejoined the United Nations Special Committee on Palestine, and flew with them to Germany and Austria, where we talked with some of the 250,000 DPs who were waiting for the world to give them an answer. UNSCOP gave them the answer in Geneva. In a majority report, the UN committee voted to partition Palestine into a Jewish state and an Arab state. The city of Jerusalem, with its holy places sacred to three great faiths, was to be held in trusteeship under the United Nations.

While the committee was writing its report, I flew to Paris and Marseille. From Marseille, it is an hour by taxi to the little harbor town of Port-de-Bouc.

Were it not for the tragedy of the 4,500 people afloat in the blistering heat, the wharf might have taken on all the aspects of a Bogart spy picture. I don't know what a spy looks like, but the people sitting in the run-down bistros and cafés along the water-front had all the postures of movie spies. A man would slouch low on his chair, with a hat pulled rakishly over one eye, pretending to sleep but obviously missing nothing. Every car was carefully observed. Every newcomer was instantly cataloged.

As you drove through the main street you made a sharp right turn to the wharf, which had little launches tied to it. Paralleling the wharf on the right was a good broad road for trucks. To the right of that was a line of trees, then another broad road for cars, and finally the typical Mediterranean waterfront street with its cafés and hotels and run-down houses. There was a rope blocking the first good broad road. The rope, I was told later, was to keep spies away from the wharf. But you could get to the wharf down the other roads, so the rope was mostly psychological and deterred nobody.

There were two cafés important to the fate of the Jews on the prison ships. One was a café, Le Provençale, at the very end of the wharf; the British used this one. It was owned by an old, fat Frenchwoman who worked it with her daughter, an attractive but utterly distraught young girl. Both women were going rapidly mad with the boom that had hit Port-de-Bouc. For the *Exodus* prison ships had brought the attention of the world to the little village. There were 1,500 people on each of the three ships, more than in the town, where some three thousand lived. All the town's activity now centered around the people floating beyond the breakwater. The French proprietress had apparently never before had so much business.

The British consul, the British correspondents, and visitors all sat at the three round outdoor tables; nobody ever sat inside, where the darkness and the sawdust were kind to the filth. There were three *pièces de la maison:* French ice, some run-down beer, and a new innovation in Port-de-Bouc—potato chips. You could buy a sack of potato chips for fifteen francs, and it was a common sight to see the English nibbling delicately at a chip with one hand while they held a glass of some yellow foam with the other.

The Jews and the French shared a café farther down the water-front street, in sight of the British café, but about a block away. This was called Le Commerce and had seven or eight outdoor tables. Here sat French gendarmes in bright blue uniforms and caps, some waterfront Apache characters who might be representing any power or none, an American worker for the Joint Distribution Committee, and French social workers employed by the French relief agency the Entr'aide Française. There were the Haganah boys, who wrote notes at the tables and dashed busily to the telephone in the back of the café, calling Paris, or rushing to the food launches, on which food sent from America and France was being carried out to the prison ships. Some of them wore open shirts and long trousers, others were in bathing trunks. And there were the Haganah girls, who made up a kind of Madame Defarge knitting corps. The girls were all young, in their late teens or early twenties. They wore simple cotton blouses and skirts and no makeup on their faces, fingernails, or stockingless toes. They looked like young, pale idealists, working for a cause. Some were Americans; others were refugees from Germany and Austria who spoke English with that odd mixture of Oxford overtones on a German rhythm. They were the links with the world outside this harbor. The refugees on the prison ships were now putting letters in empty tins and tossing them into motor launches. When the letters were recovered, they were given to the Haganah girls, who mailed them. Sometimes only addresses were tossed down; then the girls wrote the letters too. In between their other activities, they knitted pale pink and blue booties for the newborn babies on the prison ships.

The oddest character on the wharf was the abbé. The abbé was a large French priest with long, flowing black robes, thick glasses, dark brown hair streaked with a little gray, and heavy, oily skin. He carried a very businesslike brown-leather portfolio and hurried up and down the waterfront, picking up his flowing gown when it impeded his speed. He was often seen in the company of M. Blumel, who represented the French government and who was a leading Zionist in Paris.

During the war, the abbé had done distinguished work rescuing Jews. It was obvious that to him rescue was a pattern of life-and-death urgency. Now he was extending the pattern to the Jews on the prison ships. He helped get the French doctors on board the ships, the doctors who told the press about conditions on the ships and helped dub them "floating Auschwitzes." He worked with the Entr'aide Française and the American Jewish Joint Distribution Committee of the United Jewish Appeal. They fed the people. The British had refused to feed them as soon as they landed. The British told the French, the first day they docked, that one ship had no water and food at all for the next day, and two ships had enough food for one meal and no water at all. They told the French they hoped to starve the people off the ships. But the French officials and the abbé decided there would be no starvation in French territorial waters.

Each day food sent from America and France was loaded on food launches and taken out to the prison ships. And each evening the whole waterfront colony of agents, correspondents, British operatives, American and French social workers, Haganah boys and girls, and the abbé in his robes and heavy cross would drive back from Port-de-Bouc to the Hotel L'Arbois in Marseille. There they would sit in the cocktail lounge until midnight, watching one another suspiciously and whispering behind the backs of their hands about who was spying for whom on whom.

Meanwhile, in the most blistering summer in Marseille's history, a whole city of Jews was afloat in the prison ships. The first day I reached Port-de-Bouc, I met an American sailor who had just come off the ships, Eli Kalm, twenty-six, a slim, good-looking war veteran with curly black hair, laughing black eyes, and a swagger even in his voice. He had been one of the crew. "Me, I'm just a punk from the Bronx. But those people up there, baby, they're terrific. Every day they shave and get cleaned up; you'd think they were going to promenade down Park Avenue. You think they're blue up there? Kiddo, the guys who are blue are the English. They're the prisoners. They wanna go home. Famous paratroopers—now they're busy playing nursemaid to Jewish babies."

I wasn't sure the British would ever allow me to board the prison ships, so I asked Eli what it was like. His description was unforgettable. "Picture yourself on the New York subway. It's August, damned hot in August, and it's rush hour. They've turned off the fans, slammed the doors, and you're left standing up against each other for five weeks."

The only way to go on the ships legally was to get the permission of the British consul in charge of information, Edward Ashcroft. Mr. Ashcroft's office in Marseille told me he was at Port-de-Bouc. For hours I paced up and down the wharf between the Frenchwoman's café and Le Commerce, waiting. In the late afternoon, I saw the consul jump off a motorboat, followed by an officer wearing the famous red beret of the 6th Airborne Division. Before I could stop them, they had reached the big embassy car parked right in front of the Frenchwoman's café, like a horse tied up before its watering place.

Just as they opened the door of the car, I caught up with them and introduced myself. Ashcroft nodded at the introduction. He was a nice-looking man, bony and thin, with the black CID mustache sported by most of the police in Palestine and an expressive mouth that moved around a great deal, so that in the end you were more conscious of his mustache and teeth than of almost any other part of his face or body. He talked fast and nervously, like a man in need of a drink. He looked no more like a suave British diplomat than I did. He wore a wilted white shirt and white shorts, both of which were sadly rumpled from the heat. I want to register a disagreement with the social critics who say that only Englishmen can wear shorts and not look silly. I think the British are no exception.

But it was not Mr. Ashcroft's wilted shorts and thin thighs which stood out; it was the harassed and unhappy look on his face when I told him that I wanted to get on the ships.

"I can't let you on today," he said rapidly, and jumped into the car ready to drive off.

The officer with him was more eager to talk. "I'm the one who took Sandstrom and Simich from the United Nations committee all through these ships when they were at Haifa. We showed them everything," he said, "especially the crews' quarters."

Ashcroft was getting nervous. He slid over on the seat, opened the door, and beckoned to the officer.

The officer said, "Why don't you join us? We're having a drink in Martigues, where no one will bother us."

I was determined to see the prison ships that day. Ashcroft started up the car and smiled with nervous relief. "Well, so long, terribly sorry, don't you know, but there's nothing I can do about it today, that's the way things are," and drove away.

I left the British café and walked down the wharf street to Le Commerce. In a short while, I met a French police official in civilian clothes who agreed to take me out in the police launch, just to see the lay of the land. He took two gendarmes with him. The three men escorted me to the dock, helped me into the launch, opened the throttle, and in a few minutes we were chugging through the harbor. We saw Port-de-Bouc's normal peacetime activity; a ship was being refueled, another was being repaired.

We sailed beyond a bleak, gray-stone breakwater with a bleak gray lighthouse on top of it. A launch filled with British soldiers wearing red berets passed us. The boys were going to town on shore leave, the French gendarmes explained. Now, just inside the three-mile limit, on the ocean side of the lighthouse, we saw the ships themselves, first the *Runnymede Park*, named after the site on which Britain's Magna Carta had been signed. Some three hundred yards away stood the *Ocean Vigour*; and about seven hundred yards from both, the *Empire Rival*.

In the bow of each ship, taking less than a third of the deck space, was a high monkey cage with crisscrossed steel netting. On top of the cage were coils of rusted barbed wire. Inside the cage were half-naked people. Some of them waved at us, begging us to come closer. We watched in silence. The gendarmes pointed to the other two thirds of the deck, where British soldiers and crewmen were sunning themselves in bathing suits. Some of them were fishing off the deck. Near the prison ships, soldiers swam

The Runnymede Park *docked outside Port-de-Bouc in France. The British Foreign Office has decided the prison camps of Cyprus are too good for the Jews of the* Exodus. *They send the people in the three "hospital ships" to Port-de-Bouc in southern France and keep them there in unbearable heat for three weeks.*

The launch on which the friendly French gendarmes take me to the Runnymede Park.

playfully in the Mediterranean; others paddled a life raft, looking like summer vacationers on the nearby Riviera.

The atmosphere in the launch was tense. The Frenchmen looked at one another and at me and shook their heads. "We are ashamed of it," one of them said at last.

"You're not responsible," I said.

"Human beings must feel ashamed when they see any injustice."

That was it. With French conciseness, he had touched the basic truth of the tragic *Exodus* story. It was not the refugees being Jews that mattered. They could have been Indonesians or Hindus or Greeks or Turks. All around the world, man was being slaughtered, starved, threatened, enslaved. But in this little harbor, you saw the final acts of injustice. It was the moral bankruptcy of the ideals of the Magna Carta in our time that mattered; the alienation of once inalienable rights to life and liberty that we were watching through the barbed wire and iron grille. It was a grim joke, at which only the Germans on the docks at Hamburg would someday be able to laugh.

"Many of us," the Frenchman said as we circled the ships, "were in German prison camps during the war. I was in one for five years. I know who the enemy is. The people on those ships are not the enemy."

I asked one of the gendarmes if he had any objection to my taking pictures from the launch. He shrugged his shoulders. "I have none, if the others have none." I walked around the launch to the second policeman and asked him. He looked at the third gendarme and said, "It makes no difference to me, if he doesn't mind." The third gendarme shook his head. "I have no objections at all." As we were returning to the wharf, one of the gendarmes said to me, "You had better put your camera away now. There are gendarmes on the wharf."

During the long days of waiting for Mr. Ashcroft to decide whether I might board the ships, I kept traveling between Le Commerce and the Hotel L'Arbois, trying to piece together what had happened when the prison ships arrived.

There had been a government crisis over the *Exodus*. It had an odd parallel with the case of the thousand refugees whom President Roosevelt had invited to a haven in Oswego, New York, in 1944, and whom I accompanied there. Both refugee affairs, though three years apart, had caused a serious Cabinet split. In France, Foreign Minister Bidault, under pressure from Bevin, had insisted that the people must be forced off the ships, willingly or not. Minister of the Interior Dupré refused; Marseille, he said, was not Haifa; there would be no use of force in France's waters; there would be no broken skulls. In America, the State Department and the Justice Department had argued that the Oswego refugees must be sent back to Europe at the end of the war; Secretary of the Interior Harold L. Ickes insisted that they stay—the hospitality of America was at stake. In the end, the Department of the Interior won out both in America and in France.

One of the Frenchmen told me that the French Cabinet had voted to offer asylum to anyone who was prepared to disembark in France. A delegation was chosen to go aboard the vessels on their arrival in Port-de-Bouc, assuring the refugees of France's hospitality. Almost everyone assumed that most of the refugees would come down willingly. Intelligence reports from Lieutenant Colonel Martin Gregson, the officer commanding troops on the prison ships, had assured the British Foreign Office in Downing Street that the Jews would land.

The colonel even had a plan. He arranged to have the *Ocean Vigour* anchored closest to shore. The "hospital ship" was considered the easiest to unload, since it carried children, women, families, and many of the sick. The *Runnymede Park* had a large number of young people who had come down at Haifa more reluctantly; they would be more difficult to unload willingly. The *Empire Rival*, last to be filled at Haifa, was considered the toughest ship of all. The colonel arranged to have the three transports anchored in the harbor in a special pattern, keeping the ships two miles apart. As soon as the first fifty people disembarked willingly from the *Ocean Vigour*, he wanted the French to put them into a motor launch and parade them in front of the two other ships. Such an exhibit, he was sure, would be sufficient to get all the people moving.

The prefect from Marseille, the health and immigration authorities, the abbé, M. Blumel, and an interpreter went aboard the first ship. The Cabinet announcement was read to the people in French, Yiddish, and Hebrew. The people stood up and said,

"We thank the French government, which has shown the world how to deal with refugees. But *chez nous, à Palestine. Égalité, Fraternité, Liberté, mais chez nous à Palestine. Veni, veni, chez nous. Vous verez quel beau pays nous avons vis. Nous l'avons vis pendant vingt-quatre heures. Plus tarde nous arrivons. Nous n'avons rien à perdu.*"* The whole ship applauded and sang "Hatikvah."

I was told how one of the French officials walked through the hold, stepping over the people who were lying on the slimy floor. He saw a woman who had given birth a few hours before the ships arrived, still resting on the floor covered with blood. Her baby was wrapped in a rag torn from the woman's dirty dress. The woman was crying. The French official touched her shoulder and asked her why she was crying. Did she want to go to a hospital? He would see that she was taken there right away. She shook her head. "I'm crying because I'm afraid they're going to force me off the ship. I won't go down. Don't let them make me go down."

No one came off the first ship. Colonel Gregson changed his plan. He told the prefect, "Come back at three o'clock today. We'll have a thousand refugees for you. Tomorrow you can come back for the second ship and the third day for the third ship." But the prefect said he didn't have three days' time. He wanted to get it all done today.

He returned in the afternoon. The French and British officials traveled in their launch to the second ship. Again no one came down. As they left, Colonel Gregson said to the Frenchmen, "There's no point in visiting the *Empire Rival* today." The prefect insisted.

Meanwhile, the British officials on the *Empire Rival* had picked up anchor and moved several miles away. The prefect and his party chased the *Empire Rival* for two hours, until at last the transport stopped and the French launch approached it. Looking up, the officials saw bedsheets and white underwear pushed through the holes in the barbed-wire cages and weighted down

*It means: "Come, come to Palestine, our country of Equality, Fraternity, and Liberty. You will see what a beautiful country we have. In twenty-four hours, we will arrive and you will see our country. We have nothing to lose."

with lipstick tubes. On the sheets, printed in gentian violet and blue ink and lipstick, were signs:

A NOUS LA PALESTINE
LIBERTÉ, ÉGALITÉ, FRATERNITÉ

WE THANK FRANCE BUT TELL ENGLAND
TO GET US OUT OF HERE

WE WILL GO ASHORE IN EUROPE ONLY AS DEAD MEN

The Frenchmen and the English officials climbed aboard the *Rival* and stopped short. A strange thing was happening. The flag, the yellow quarantine flag, began to go down the flagpole, and they saw the blue-and-white flag of Zion with the interlocked triangles of the Star of David slowly rising.

They learned later that it was a flag with a history. It was the flag that the American friends of the Haganah had given the crew in Baltimore. After the battle of the *Exodus*, a seventeen-year-old boy who had lived in the Kloster-Indersdorf DP orphanage with Hirsch Yakubovich dipped the flag in Hirsch's blood. He wrapped the flag around his body. The soldiers frisked him in the search pen on the Haifa dock, but didn't find it. He hid it all during the long ten-day voyage back to France and on the night before arrival, he climbed to the top of the masthead with the flag wrapped around his body and waited. He stayed through the night and all during the hot morning of the next day, waiting, without food and water. Other boys tried to call him down; he refused. In the early afternoon, they went up after him and forced him down. A few hours later he saw the French launch approaching. He scrambled up to the masthead, tied the flag securely to the mast, and held it out so that everyone could see. He had a trumpet around his neck. With the flag waving, he blew the first notes of "Hatikvah." The whole ship began to sing.

The French delegation knew now that no one would come down. They left the *Rival*, with the signs on the barbed-wire cages waving in the sun. À NOUS LA PALESTINE. LIBERTÉ, ÉGALITÉ, FRATERNITÉ.

Nothing English ever happens without the weather. First Port-de-Bouc suffered the worst heat in its history. The British were sure the heat would force the people off the ships. The heat failed. Then the rains came. For four solid days, the skies boiled over. The rain slashed against the prison ships; they shook with the rumble of thunder. No one could stay outdoors in the prison cages and on each ship 1,500 people had to crowd into the holds below. The water streamed through the grilles above the holds, and there was no tarpaulin. The 1,500 prisoners on each ship couldn't lie down; there wasn't enough room in the holds for all their bodies. They stood up against one another day and night, trying to keep the water off their bodies; some of the luckier ones huddled against the walls. But they could huddle there only at night. During the day, the walls grew too hot and their bodies felt scalded. They stood packed against each other.

The British were certain the storm would succeed where the sun had failed. The people would surely crack now and leave the prison ships. But they still did not understand their prisoners. On the *Runnymede Park* a group of leaders approached Captain Barclay, requesting that he grant shelter in empty storage rooms to the people who had been flooded out. A dialogue between the prisoners, Colonel Gregson, Captain Barclay, and an army captain, written down immediately after the conference, shows the kind of reports which the British sent to Downing Street, on the basis of which Foreign Secretary Bevin made policy for the *Exodus*.

LEADER OF JEWS: In these rains, some three hundred of us have no shelter. When these people go below in the holds, the added congestion is almost unbearable for any length of time. We ask you to afford additional space for them.

BRITISH: There is no additional space. Moreover the French coast is very near and anyone who desires can disembark.

LEADER OF JEWS: We've heard this refrain many times already. You should know by now that the refugees will not disembark under any circumstances.

BRITISH: The majority of the refugees are willing to disembark but you are preventing them by force. It is clear that you were lying when you declared in the presence of a French reporter that everyone was free to decide for himself whether to get off the ship or not.

LEADER OF JEWS: Let me restate emphatically that the Jews are remaining aboard and refusing to disembark of their own volition and as a result of their own individual decisions and understanding. I am quite prepared to be arrested, or transferred to another vessel, together with the other committee representatives, and then you will be convinced that the immigrants' refusal to leave the ship is their own free decision.

BRITISH: I repeat that you will return neither to Palestine

nor to Cyprus. A long and difficult voyage awaits you if you do not land here. Only suffering awaits you. Seize this opportunity of French magnanimity and disembark.

LEADER OF JEWS: This is not news for us. We all know this song and we are sick of hearing it again. Have you anything new to tell us?

BRITISH: There is no additional space for you.

LEADER OF JEWS: We will manage. Thank you very much. But don't delude yourself that the rains will help you.

The people sitting at Le Commerce, sipping beer in the shade, could not stop talking about the weird courage of the people on the ships, their will not to come off.

Pilgrimages to Palestine were not new. In the Middle Ages, the Crusaders had put a cross on their armor and marched south and east. Now the Jews, with the flag of Zion, were marching south and east again. The reasons had changed, but not the pattern. They were not necessarily religious Jews, though there were some religious and Orthodox Jews among them. They were Jews to whom the language of Zion was a signpost and the history of Zion a goal.

To the Christians, to whom the word *Jew* had always been mystical and strange, the Jew of the *Exodus* was the weirdest Jew of all. He was the Jew who refused to die in the gas chambers, the Jew who refused to wait in the DP camps while the world argued over him or forgot him; the Jew who was unafraid of the armed might of Britain.

The stories about the people behind the cages were like the creation of a saga; you could almost feel the birth of a new epic as the French and Jewish café dwellers talked about the eighteen-year-old girl who had stones in her kidney. The doctor, who was deadening her pain with morphine, told her he couldn't go on drugging her indefinitely. She would have to get off and go to a hospital. The girl refused. "I'll die here, but I won't go down."

One of the Haganah girls stopped her knitting to tell me, with the air of someone reciting a case history, of the woman who needed an emergency appendectomy. There were Swiss doctors from the International Red Cross as well as French doctors and refugee doctors on the ships now. One of the doctors told the woman, "You must go to a hospital onshore. I cannot operate on you on the ship. There are no sheets, no blankets, no anesthesia, no water, no way of making the place sterile. You may die here."

The woman was impressed by his earnestness. But she had one more question. "If I go down to the hospital in Marseille, will I be allowed to come back on the ship when my appendix is out?"

The doctor, who feared for the woman's life, went to the British authorities with her question. Their answer was no. Anyone who left the ships could not return. The woman refused to go ashore.

Everyone loved the jovial white-bearded man who had said, "I'm eighty years old. My wife is with me; we've been married fifty-seven years. Look, the two of us have survived Russian hell, Polish hell, German hell. We'll survive British hell too."

One afternoon, walking down Marseille's Cannebière, which the American sailors pronounced "can o'beer" and took their pronunciation literally, Eli Kalm, the sailor from the Bronx, added his favorite anecdote to my list. Already the *Exodus* was losing reality, becoming a phantom ship on which the weird people of history were creating a new mythology.

"A kid of ten," he said, "was lying on our hospital floor coughing like mad. We all figured he was dying of TB. I said to him, 'Why don't you get off?' He told me in Yiddish, 'I lost too much health getting on the *Exodus*. You think I'll get off now?' A few days later the doctors examined him and found his TB wasn't as bad as we thought. Anyway, not too contagious. So they allowed him to stay. His parents looked upon him as a regular hero. Boy, they loved him, as proud as if they gave birth to Joan of Arc, a Jewish Joan of Arc.

"All they think about on the ships," Eli said as we walked along the Cannebière, "is when are we going? When are we getting out of here? When are we getting to Palestine? I was pretty friendly with Major Gray on the *Rival*, and he'd say to me all the time,

'Tell me, Eli, why don't they get off the ship? Why don't they do the decent thing? Our boys like them. Why do they antagonize us?'

" 'Look, Major,' I said, 'they want to go to Palestine to live, don't you understand? They're not here to like you. They'll cut your throat, if they have to, to get there. The Jews have become the fighting Jews. They're not like my Bronx Jews. They don't whine because they can't get something. They'll go on a seven-day hunger strike. They'll die, but they'll get there.' "

"What kind of people are they, Eli?" I asked him. On the horizon, a red sun was dropping fiercely into the Mediterranean.

"They're all kinds. There's one guy, he's a wealthy manufacturer from Düsseldorf. He works in the hospital. He's got a rich cousin in Tel Aviv who's a tailor. He gave Gray his cousin's address, so when Gray goes back to his post in Palestine, he'll get fixed up with a swell new uniform.

"On the *Rival* there are a lot of Hungarians," Eli said. "They've been through the works, got Auschwitz tattoo marks on their arms, but they don't talk about it. Never mention it. We got one guy who was in Russia all during the war. He's got those big Red Army leather boots they wear in Siberia. Every morning you wake up, there he is taking his boots off the wall and shining them, as if he was getting ready for inspection. They used to call us Americans 'Chokoladniki,' because we like candy bars. We even had some French Moroccans and a bunch of French boulevardiers who always sang songs of Pig Alley. It's real city life; the only difference is they sing more than in a city. I miss them, honest. The way they kept clean on that ship! We had two latrines in a cage and six holes in each latrine. No running water, just a trickle of salt water to take the refuse out to sea. They have little basins in front of the latrines where they do their laundry, and then they hang all the wash on the barbed wire. The British can't do a thing with them. They turn a jail into a backyard for the kids' diapers. The kids are washed before they wash themselves. Some of those Hungarian women were beautiful—and boy did they keep themselves clean! Spotless, honest. Each morning, with what little we had on that ship, they'd fix themselves up so you'd think they were going for a walk down Fifth Avenue. Maybe you heard about their being promiscuous on the ship? Don't believe it, honey. They're the most moral people you ever met in your life. You know how we slept on those ships, one body up against another one. I got a couple of swift kicks for getting a little too close to one gal I was interested in. And just a couple of days ago, before I came off, we were supposed to have a wedding. The girl called the wedding off because she said there was no privacy.

"Remember that play in New York, *Jacobowsky and the Colonel*? These people are all Jacobowskys. Wherever they see a ditch, they jump in. They accept everything, but they'll go on fighting to get there. It's a life of despair mixed with terrific hope—life gets tough, just start singing. Every time they'd come up to me and say, 'Chokoladnik, what's new?'

" 'What's new?' I'd say. 'You know. Nothing's new.'

"It didn't depress them. They'd shrug their shoulders, or make a little joke about how it's worse on the soldiers, how we've screwed them up too. These are Bible people, stubborn, stiff-necked. And what a joy in life! The only thing that gets them down is when they start thinking that nobody cares what the hell is happening to them. It's hot up there, it's hot as a son of a bitch. You stay in the harbor and the sun beats down on you all day and it never cools off, even at night. A few hundred who are lucky sleep on the deck in the cage. But everybody who sleeps on the grilles keeps the air out for the thousand and more in the hold down below. The royal suite is right on top of the two latrines. Each night about ten people are lucky: they get to sleep on each latrine. Each night some women faint in the hold. They're carried to the hospital to be revived, and then they're helped up on deck. They're allowed to sleep on the little walk around the grille. Maybe even on the toilet.

"The British don't care how we sleep; they just don't want anybody to sleep on the latrines—afraid they'll break through. The soldiers are supposed to have as little to do with the people as possible. One night some ships appeared on our starboard side. All the people in the cage rushed over and about ten people stood up on the toilet shed to get a better look. A soldier rushed inside the cage with his gun, and pulled the bolt back as if he was forcing a bullet into the chamber. The people just laughed. They don't care anymore. The soldier ran out of the cage. He was more scared than they were. They might have ripped him apart.

"You know that every single can of food that comes aboard is punctured by a bayonet to see if there's anything in it besides food? The people laugh about it. The bomb scare. They asked an officer how he imagined a bomb could get in a tin of sardines. 'You don't know,' he said, 'people are very clever.' Meanwhile, a lot of food is spoiled by the bayoneting."

From Eli, from other American crew members who had come off the ships and were now waiting for passage home, and from the sick refugees who were taken to a hospital, I learned what an average day was like on the prison ships. The day began at six in the morning; it was not the sun which awakened you, but the heat, for it was never dark on the ships. A giant searchlight played on the faces of those who slept in the outside cage, while huge bare lights fell on the people's faces all night in the holds. The prison guards walking up and down the duckwalks above the grille could watch everything that went on below. There was neither privacy nor silence. Harry Weinsaft, one of the crew members who had come off the *Ocean Vigour*, told me that the duckwalk patrol was silent, but most of the time the soldiers walked on the grille itself, making a clattering noise that kept people awake most of the night.

"You must know about these prison ships. It's one of the ironies of history," Uri Urmacher, who had survived the slaughter in the orphan car in Poland, told me later. "They're former Liberty ships America sent to help save the British because Nazi U-boats were decimating their fleet. The British then converted them into prison ships with these fancy names—*Empire Rival*, *Runnymede Park*—and imprisoned us in them."

It was the children who kept morale high. Floating schools were established. There were leaders of the Youth Aliyah movement, which means, literally, the Children's Immigration, perhaps the greatest movement of children since the Crusades. Thousands of orphaned children had been brought to Palestine by the Youth Aliyah. As soon as the people realized that the sojourn in Port-de-Bouc might be a long one, they began to teach the children, pretending they were already living in Palestine. The curriculum of study was work in the morning, classes in the afternoon, recreation in the evening. In the morning the boys and girls worked, helping to prepare and distribute the food. The British neither supplied the food nor cooked it nor passed it out. The refugees were on their own. Refugee cooks, assisted by the young people, cooked the food sent up by the Joint and the Entr'aide Française and distributed it. The refugees' committee divided the 1,500 people on each ship into groups of thirty or forty, into little kibbutzim, little collectives. Each group had four people who were allowed out of the cage to get the food. Since the soldiers allowed only two out at a time, each meal took about four hours.

This food was good, unlike the food on the voyage from Haifa to Port-de-Bouc, when the British had fed the people dehydrated army rations. Uri described the food: "They gave us canned food from the First World War—soup with worms in it, crackers with green fungus." Prisoners and soldiers alike fell victims to boils, rashes, eruptions, and something that was loosely called scurvy. Now each morning the young students under the training of the Youth Aliyah helped line up the people while a woman doctor, sent aboard by the French, painted everyone with gentian violet. It was a kind of war paint. Sometimes a whole head was covered with it, hair and all, sometimes a whole face, or arms or back or legs.

Some of the people's skins were pocked and pitted for life, but some were cured, and the cure, like the cause, was attributed to the food. Certainly the food sent aboard by the Americans and the French was better food than many of the people had eaten since before the war. Stacked up in the warehouse behind Le Commerce, the food looked like an international harvest. Signs printed on wooden crates told a story of international relief—IRISH STEWED STEAK (which came from America); CORNED BEEF from the Argentine; FRENCH SARDINES in olive oil; French and American EVAPORATED MILK; and even something from Palestine—ASSIS JAM.

Each day young Jewish volunteers on the wharf filled the food launches high with crates of fresh pears, sacks of long white French bread, onions, potatoes, and even books.

In the afternoon, the schools functioned like regular schools. On good days, classes were held on the deck of the cage in front of the latrine. Older people took turns teaching. Mostly they taught the Hebrew language and literature and the biblical story of the Exodus from Egypt. If the children shut their eyes, they could forget the smell was of latrines, forget that they were in a monkey cage with British soldiers watching, and that the hills in the distance were those of southern France. For a little while they could dream that the smell was of olive trees and orange groves, and they were in the hills of Israel.

Each evening at seven, a space was cleared in the crowded hold, a kind of bullring. The huge, glaring, unshaded lights burned down on the faces of the weary and the strong, of the old warriors and the children. Each evening, they made a Parliament of displaced persons. They made a Parliament with leaders and citizens, where they discussed the daily problems of their own prison world, which had reality, and the unreal world outside the prison which had forgotten them. They made a town hall, where they voiced their convictions and their fears. In the evening, they were one people. They no longer resented one another with a thousand years of national hatreds, of Hungarians hating Poles and Poles hating Germans. They were one people. They were a musical people, and they missed the accordions and the guitars which the British had confiscated at Haifa. A few of them had hidden their harmonicas, and now the musicians drew closer to the center of the bullring, and an orchestra of harmonicas played the songs these people loved. Sometimes they played the songs of the partisans, and the songs of the ghetto. But mostly they played the new songs of Palestine, and the song which had great meaning to them, the song which said, "Israel Lives."

Faces were always scrubbed for the Parliament, and the children looked spotless. They had no change of clothing, but on each ship there was some woman who stayed awake most of the night washing. On the *Ocean Vigour*, it was a young bride of twenty-one, who had led one hundred Hungarian orphans onto the *Exodus*. While the people slept, she and a few other women scrubbed the little dresses and the ragged little shorts in the bowls outside the latrines, and hung them on the barbed-wire fence of the cage to dry. And each evening, the filth and sweat of the hold seemed to disappear, because the children sang in the center of the bullring as if it were a holiday.

These were a people with high respect for learning and the cultural leader on the *Ocean Vigour* was a thirteen-year-old boy, Yankele, who became the leader because he could recite Bialik and the great and tragic poems written in the Warsaw ghetto and in the death camps. In the Parliament of Peoples, Yankele, at thirteen, was the most respected person on the ship.

Of all the things that were done to the people, nothing seemed as grim to them as when the British burned the books brought to them in the food launches. Afraid of books as propaganda, the officer commanding troops on the *Empire Rival* ordered that all books in Hebrew and Yiddish be burned. Among the books was the Bible. These were the people of the Bible; it was the book which they had given to Christianity and the world; it was the book which had kept them alive and integrated as a people. Now their book was burned on the prison ship. In the Parliament, in the bullring in the evening, they sat silently, mourning the book as if a person had died. They were the People of the Book and of the Land, and on this prison ship both had been taken from them.

Once again, as when they had been separated from their families on the dock at Haifa, panic struck. They called a hunger strike for twenty-four hours. The launch carrying their rations was returned to shore. They refused to accept their food. They told their pregnant women and their sick people and their children not to fast. The women and the children and the sick refused and joined the strike.

The French police and the representatives of the health department went out in their motor launches to the prison ships.

Mass choruses shouted to them, "We will not come down. We will not come down. We will come down only in Palestine."

On the *Ocean Vigour*, the people strung up signs in English and French: OPEN THE DOORS OF PALESTINE, OUR ONLY HOPE.

They smuggled telegrams off the ships to the prefect: HOW CAN YOU ALLOW THE ENGLISH TO TREAT US IN SUCH AN INHUMAN WAY ON THIS NAZI SHIP?

They were convinced that no one cared; they were sure that the conscience of the world had gone dead. "Our feeling is," someone wrote in a letter that was smuggled down to us, "our feeling is, and this depresses us more than all else, that with time the world has grown used to this phenomenon which is known as *Exodus 1947*. While for us it is a question of our lives."

To cheer the people up, Avi, a representative of the Mossad on the shore, sent a letter to the refugees aboard the ship.

Dear Comrades!

Our plan has succeeded. The French press has woken from its slumber and returned to the fact that there are Jews on the French coast who have not only refused to succumb mentally to their conditions on their Auschwitz ships, but who can also take action, if necessary.

It made a tremendous impression when boats with food returned to Port-de-Bouc without having unloaded their cargo. They couldn't believe their ears about your refusal to take your daily food rations. The "rats" [the code name for the British] were even more impressed by your fast. Their consul got on the ships to obtain information about conditions and when he got off he was so incensed he issued a denial, that is, as if there had been no hunger strike last night. The French authorities have also begun working to bring the matter to their government's attention, and today put the three forgotten ships back on the front page.

It must be said that now, for the first time, the American press began taking a systematic interest in their fate. The

New York Herald Tribune sent one of its top journalists, Ruth Gruber, who was the first journalist sent by that paper to cover the UN committee inquiry into Eretz Israel, and also covered the Anglo-American commission of inquiry a year ago. She understands us well and her articles have special importance. Last night she tried to obtain permission to board the ships from the consul of "rats," and he refused. She did manage to get to the vicinity of the ships and take photographs. Maybe she will get permission yet to board. Meanwhile this action has succeeded, that is, people are again taking an interest in your fate and we need to be prepared (to assure) that that interest does not wane until the ships sail. What is clear now is that neither the "rats" nor other people understood until now what strength these Jews have after all they went through. And the "rats" have made not a few mistakes because of their mistaken evaluation of your condition.

We embrace you with the assurance that we shall continue with this war with our combined strength until we achieve our goal of immigrating to Eretz Israel and turning it into a free homeland for a free people.

The British took the next step. They announced to the world from Paris that there was no hunger strike. When that news broke to us on the dock at Port-de-Bouc the next morning, after the refugees had been floating in the sun for three weeks and we had watched the food launches come back unloaded and the French doctors aboard had seen the people refuse to take food, a French journalist bit his lip and said, "This is the biggest lie since Goebbels's death."

I went to call on M. Albert Mallet, the *chef du cabinet* of the prefecture at Marseille. M. Mallet said that he had received a telegram smuggled off the ships. The message told of the hunger strike, and invited the prefect to come aboard to see conditions for himself.

I could not resist telling him that I admired France's attitude. He leaned across his neat desk and, speaking rapidly in French, said, "France will not force anybody to disembark, but we will offer asylum and hospitality to anybody who wishes to land. We are feeding the people. We have inoculated them against diseases. We have taken off all the cases of measles and the serious case of spinal meningitis. We have sent the convalescents to Paris. But our position is absolutely not to force anyone off the ships. France understands the attitude of the refugees."

I queried him about some of the messages from the ships which had pointed out to the French that by allowing the British ships to linger, the French were really playing into Britain's hands and prolonging the suffering of the refugees. Did he agree with that? And had the French given the British any deadline for clearing out of the harbor?

"We know nothing whatsoever of the intentions of the British," he said. "Nor have we given them any time limit. In accordance with our concepts of hospitality, we can't say to the British ships, 'Well, you've been here long enough. Now get out of here.' After all, the ships are in French territorial waters. All that we could do was to have our government call the attention of the British government to the dangers of disease and epidemics breaking out, so long as the ships lie here. But up to now, we've had no knowledge whatsoever of the intentions of the British. I believe"—he spoke with great diplomatic caution—"that the French government may have intervened with the British government by asking that the ships be removed."

From other sources, less diplomatic and official, I learned that Bidault had made three representations to the British, asking that the ships be removed from French territorial waters. As foreign minister, M. Bidault could not help but regret this irritant in Anglo-French relations, which was causing a wave of indignation against the British. One of the French dailies said that relations had not been as strained since the Syrian war in 1945, when the British maneuvered to get the French out of Syria and Lebanon. The Quai d'Orsay was particularly unhappy that the problem had come up on the eve of three-power talks on the Ruhr, when M. Bidault needed Mr. Bevin's help against the United States.

But the disagreements between the Ministry of the Interior and the Ministry of Foreign Affairs in France had been ironed out and Bidault had signed a note, couched in friendly language, asking the British to conclude *"l'affaire Exodus."* Apparently, the British Foreign Office had never answered the note. Bidault was even more embarrassed, because after a meeting with the British ambassador, Alfred Duff Cooper, he announced to the National Assembly that the British were going to take the people to a port under British jurisdiction. Bidault gave no date, but the impression was that action would be taken immediately. After that announcement, there were no further political discussions, but now, with the hunger strike, the *Exodus* was once more in a prominent place on the desk of the French president.

Back at Port-de-Bouc, I walked up and down the wharf, talking to a sick man who had just been carried down and who lay on a low hospital mattress in the courtyard behind the offices of the Entr'aide Française. The offices were in a girls' school, which the French relief society had taken over. Now it was an infirmary run by French doctors, a kind of annex for the *Exodus*.

The sick man told me he had been running a high temperature for a week. It was only when his breathing had become almost unbearable that he had consented to go to the hospital in Marseille. He was waiting now for the ambulance to take him there.

"During our hunger strike yesterday," he told me, "I said to the soldiers on the ship, 'I must go up on deck. I must get air.' But the soldiers just sat at the hospital door with their Sten guns and said, 'No, you can't go up. We have orders.' "

On his prison ship, all movements were restricted during the hunger strike, and all privileges revoked. Families were not allowed to visit their relatives in the sick bay, and no one was allowed out of the cage.

"What do you intend to do now?" I asked him.

"I want to go to the hospital, and as soon as I'm cured, I want to go to Palestine. I only ask that they cure me enough so I can live to make the voyage."

While we waited for the British to confirm or deny the Paris embassy story of the hunger strike, I talked to the two French doctors to whom the refugees were most indebted for the fact that no serious epidemics had broken out aboard the ships: Dr. Jean Gayla, General Inspector of Public Health, a tall, striking man, and Dr. Jacques Besson, young and intense, the representative of the Assistance Publique de Marseille. They had been tireless since the first day the ships arrived; they brought medical supplies on board; they had the sick patients carried down; they took a variety of blood tests which were analyzed in a laboratory set up in the school. When four cases of measles broke out on the *Empire Rival*, they sent a doctor and two nurses who spent two days and nights vaccinating all the children between one and thirteen. They worked with the Swiss doctors, and though they were medical men and not political men, they made a report on the number of people who had disembarked from the twenty-ninth of July to the twenty-first of August which became a highly political report. They showed that the number had grown smaller regularly and that in that three weeks' period, of the 4,500 people, a total of only 159 had come down.

"Conditions on the ships are not very good," Dr. Gayla told me. "In the holds all the masses are pushed together. It is very dangerous for their health. We expect fifty births within the next two weeks. The JDC and the Entr'aide Française are sending us fifty layettes."

These fifty babies would be British subjects.

Outside the courtyard, rumors began to spread across the tables of Le Commerce that the ships would leave before Sunday. Someone said the ships had taken on a new supply of coal. Someone else said they had loaded 150 tons of food during the night. There were no soldiers on leave in the streets of Port-de-Bouc or Martigues. A telephone call from Rome told us Rome had heard a report that the ships were leaving immediately, heading straight for Germany. We refused to believe that rumor. Ashcroft had told one of the correspondents some days before that the people would "definitely not" be taken to Germany. Though we realized that Ashcroft was not necessarily in the confidence of the policy-makers, we were inclined to agree with him.

The rumors grew hotter. Someone denied now that 150 tons of food had been loaded. But someone else swore that the British were taking away the refugees' food and storing it for a long journey. The British had barred all volunteer workers on the food launches from the prison ships; only two French workers were allowed to unload the supplies. A man with dark glasses walked past me at Le Commerce, where everyone watched everyone else, and whispered to me out of the side of his mouth, "The British consul is on the ships and is telling the people, 'Come down now or you will go to jail!'"

Suddenly someone said, "He's come off the ships." I hurried to the Frenchwoman's café in time to see Ashcroft running to his car. "Is it true?" I asked him.

"Yes, we've been on all the boats. On the *Ocean Vigour* we have had a declaration." Then, without a note in his hand, even punctuating the declaration for me, he told me what one of the leaders, a Polish lawyer, had said. "Quote, The immigrants on the *Ocean Vigour* have no hostility for the British people or the British government, full stop. We have, above all, no hostility toward the escort, or the officials of the ship, who have treated us with humanity, full stop. We will not disembark, but we will not in any way offend against the good relations which exist between us, the British escort, and the crew, full stop. We put our trust in the democratic feeling of the British government and we do not believe that while we are under British control, anything serious can happen to us, full stop, end quote."

When I commented that he had a remarkable memory, Mr. Ashcroft said, "I wrote it down, young woman." The important thing was not the statement but the people. Had any of them come down? None, Mr. Ashcroft said. "The Polish doctor of laws had a drink with Colonel Gregson and said he hoped the British government would not be hostile to the Zionists. We said we knew that the British Labour government would not be hostile; we were there in the role of arbiters."

The story of how the ultimatum was delivered on the ships was told us by a special information officer who had been sent down from the Paris embassy—Donald Mallet. It was odd that he had the same name as the French *chef du cabinet*. Sitting on a table in a smoke-filled room of the café Le Provençale, Mr. Mallet told us, "This morning, Mr. Sidney Entwhistle Kay, the British consul general in Marseille, Lieutenant Colonel Gregson, and I went to Port-de-Bouc to announce the decision taken by the British government. At eleven A.M. we went aboard the *Runnymede Park*. The leaders of the refugees were received on deck by the consular party and they were informed through an interpreter of this decision. British soldiers distributed a leaflet among the passengers."

Mr. Mallet did not tell us what the leaflet said, but I saw one which had been smuggled off the ships. Typewritten in English and French, the ultimatum read, "To the passengers on the *Runnymede Park*, *Empire Rival*, *Ocean Vigour*: This announcement is made to you on behalf of the British Government.

"Those of you who do not begin to disembark at Port-de-Bouc before 18 o'clock (6:00) P.M. tomorrow, August 22nd, will be taken by sea to Hamburg."

The announcement was written on the ship's blackboard in German, Yiddish, and Polish, to make certain that it was understood by everyone. "A Pole and a German protested the policy of the British government," Mallet said. "When they finished talking, the refugees applauded and began singing the national anthem.

"We left the first ship and at eleven-oh-three boarded the *Empire Rival* and went through the same procedure. The representatives of the refugees were two Americans, who received our announcement and simply replied, 'Okay.' "

The American boys were still throwing in their lot with the refugees. They had had all these weeks to come down. I thought of the American crew talking to me at midnight in Haifa, of Dov Miller from Brooklyn who had become a leader of the refugees and of Bill Bernstein who was dead. Now the ultimatum had been delivered and the boys had made no heroic speeches. Simply "Okay."

"At twelve-fifteen," Mr. Mallet went on, "our party boarded the *Ocean Vigour* and made the same announcement. The refugee leaders asked leave to talk with the people, take a vote, and give the boarding party the people's reply. In half an hour the Polish lawyer entered the cabin and announced, 'Our decision is not to disembark.' "

Mallet shortened the speech that Ashcroft had dictated to me. The refugees—he quoted the lawyer—had decided to maintain order and not make any demonstrations. "We trust the democratic traditions of the British government."

Mallet told us the ships would put in first at Gibraltar for fuel and supplies. Then they would proceed to Hamburg. The correspondents pressed him. "Will force be used?"

He answered with some hesitation, "I don't know."

That night, Haganah issued a declaration saying:

This time our power has not been sufficient to land the Exodus immigrants on the shore of our homeland. But we shall do all in our power to return the Exodus immigrants to Palestine in the near future. The stand taken by the immigrants in their struggle has written a brilliant page in the history of the Jews' fight for their freedom. The work of bringing the Jews back to their homeland will continue and be intensified. We are convinced that the entire civilized world condemns this latest crime of the British Government.

During that soul-searching night, when no one slept on the ships, two Haganah boats approached and through loudspeakers told the people that they were not alone, that people all over the world had heard of their heroism and would fight their fight. The English turned on the sirens and drowned out the voice of the Haganah.

Now the British had no more excuse to keep me off the ships. A few days after the hunger strike, they had promised to take aboard a representative of the British press and a representative of the French press, and I was to represent the American press. We waited for hours at the rendezvous, but the consul failed to appear. Now, the last day the ships were in port, Ashcroft and Mallet announced that the press would be allowed on board. A Reuters man arrived from Paris; we learned that the British had phoned Paris asking that the *Daily Mail* and Reuters be represented. We were to meet Ashcroft and Mallet on the wharf at one. At two in the afternoon, they were still not there, and sometime later we saw them strolling down the hot wharf road with the *Daily Mail* man. We rushed to join them.

Ashcroft jumped into a French motor launch and beckoned to two men and me to climb in after him. Even on the last day, relations between the French and British were stretched to the breaking point. A Frenchman yelled at him, "You can't commandeer this boat."

Ashcroft spluttered, "I'm the British consul."

"I don't care who you are. You tried the same thing yesterday. Do the French people have no more rights?"

The argument continued while the world press watched with some amusement. In the end, Ashcroft herded us off the launch and led us to another boat. He divided the press, so that Mallet took some aboard the *Ocean Vigour*, while he led the others to the *Runnymede Park*. I was assigned to Ashcroft's group. I noticed he was carrying the typewriter and raincoat of the Reuters man.

The harbor was unexpectedly rough; the launch bounced and rolled through the water, tossing us wildly against one another. We climbed over the oil drum in the rocking boat and clung to the Jacob's ladder clumsily, as it swung high against the hull of the *Runnymede Park*. Ashcroft introduced us to Lieutenant Colonel Martin Gregson, the British officer commanding the troops aboard the three transports. Gregson was a tanned, broad-faced, pipe-smoking Englishman who had a constant grin on his face and never a doubt in his brain. He seemed to be in his middle thirties and apparently had wasted little time in learning where life's pleasures lay. He looked like the type that has no use for the Labour government except for its policy on Palestine. He greeted us with an amused smile, as if we had caught him with a towel around his midriff ready to take a bath. He shook the hand of the Reuters correspondent and let a dark, unpleasant secret out of the bag. "So you're the one who's making the trip with us. I hope you find it gay." The Reuters man looked as if he were going to be seasick. We understood why Ashcroft himself had carried the correspondent's typewriter and raincoat. They were smuggling him aboard. We learned a little later that "the highest Foreign Office official," obviously Bevin himself, had requested that an English news agency man and no one else be allowed to make the trip. Maurice Pearlman, one of the correspondents, asked Ashcroft outright if he could go too. Ashcroft said unhappily, "I'm afraid not."

"Then why are you allowing Reuters to go?"

Poor Ashcroft brushed his CID mustache jerkily. "After all, Reuters is the official government news agency."

"What?" the whole press shouted at once. Reuters had just spent about a million dollars trying to convince the world that it was *not* the official government agency.

"Reuters would be very unhappy," Pearlman said, "to hear you call it the official agency."

Ashcroft was distraught. "Well, you know"—he tried to smile—"official, I mean, the way Tass is not the official Soviet news agency."

Of course, every reporter knew that Tass was the official Soviet news agency, and some of the press smirked openly at his remark.

Grinning and a little impatient now, with one foot in his cabin and one foot on the deck, Colonel Gregson waited for us to ask him our questions and leave him alone. This was the man in charge of all the troops, the man who sent the intelligence reports from the ships to Downing Street, the man of whom we should be asking the searching questions, the policy questions: What did the *Exodus* mean? What did the month in Port-de-Bouc add up to? What did Britain plan to do? But no one asked them. All you could ask of this grinning officer were the black-

and-white facts, the statistics that filled out a story, like "Colonel, how many babies were born on board the ships in Port-de-Bouc?" His answer even to that was casual and airy. "I don't know. Put down any number you want, maybe six, maybe a dozen, maybe twenty. They're always having babies." His trailing laughter seemed to mock us good-naturedly for wanting an accurate answer to such a fluid question.

It was typical of the whole tragedy of this prison ship that such a man, detached and amused, should be the commander, while behind his cabin in an iron cage, a trapped people were clamoring for us to see them in their last hour.

All around us stood the prison guard and the motley crew. Eight Egyptian Arabs had quit in disgust. They had been hired, they said, for a commercial sea voyage, not for a floating Devil's Island. The soldiers were envious; they too had been misled—like the refugees. They too had thought they were taking an overnight trip to Cyprus and had brought no extra clothing with them. They felt filthy and foul and homesick. Their respect for themselves had deteriorated. In a sense they were more frustrated and demoralized than the refugees; they weren't Jacobowskys.

They watched the press with mixed emotions. They knew we had heard the stories of the "incidents" between the troops and refugees and the story of the burning of the books. In the beginning, they had been friendly, but as the journey continued and they too fell victim to rashes and boils, they began to push the children around, refused to let them out of the cages on the free deck, and slammed the cages shut. When French launches motored near the ships, they would shout down, "You dirty French b——s; you deserted us at Dunkerque."

Looking at the soldiers now, some of them no older than high school students, I remembered Dr. Chaim Weizmann saying to me in his study in Rehovot, "Everybody carries anti-Semitism in his haversack." The haversack of the soldiers had spilled. Theirs was a thankless job; the only break in the monotony came from locking and unlocking the wire cage.

We talked to a few of the soldiers, and then left Colonel Gregson and Mr. Ashcroft to drink their last drink in the colonel's cabin. Our escort was a young, quiet captain from the 6th Airborne Division. He led us slowly in the hot sun to the fore section of the bridge.

Below us was the cage. Squeezed between a green toilet shed and some steel plates were hundreds and hundreds of half-naked people who looked as though they had been thrown together into a dog pound. For a moment I had the hideous feeling that they were barking. Trapped and lost, they were shouting at us in all languages, shattering one another's words. Some pressed their faces against the slanted fencing and their bodies looked broken and distorted. We watched the cage grow tighter and wilder as more people forced their way from somewhere in the bowels of the ship and pushed against the people already inside the narrow cage.

Most of the people shouting at me were young men and a few young women with determined faces, eager to defy the great British Empire. Some leaned against the improvised two-door outhouse, the only toilet for the 1,500 prisoners aboard the ship.

Among the faces were those of the beautiful women I had seen at Haifa, with the wide-set green eyes and high Hungarian cheekbones. There were also the strong faces, filled with determination, of men getting ready for battle. Most of the men wore shorts, held up with a belt or a piece of string. Their chests and feet were naked. Their rashes were covered with streaks of gentian violet.

The women wore cotton dresses; some wore only brassieres and shorts. Several had cloths over their heads for protection from the sun. There was a touch of loveliness in the cage; a little girl wearing a white cotton petticoat had a white ribbon in her soft hair.

"May we enter the cage?" a French journalist asked our officer escort.

He shook his head.

"May we ask questions?"

"Go ahead."

"Do you want to get off the ship?" the journalist shouted at the refugees.

The cage rocked with their answer. Only the word "no" was comprehensible; the rest was babel. In French, German, Yiddish, Hebrew, Hungarian, English, they scolded us, blamed us, waved their fists at us.

One man shouted loudest. As he spoke, the others cried, "Sh-sh-sh," until there was silence. "We will not come down," he screamed. "We will come down willingly only in Palestine. Here we will come down as corpses."

We learned that this man, with his thin, naked chest, his long hair, his tense face and eyes stretched wide, was Mordecai Rosman. At Le Commerce, among the Haganah boys and the Madame Defarge knitting corps, Rosman was a legend. During the war, he had been a leader in the Warsaw ghetto. In the ghetto uprising, he had inspired the people to fight even without guns and when the uprising failed, he had led a whole group out of the ghetto to safety in the Polish woods. For the rest of the war, he had fought as a partisan leader, constantly driving his followers to new acts of daring, inflaming them to move an inch because he was determined to move a mile.

Inside the cage, he looked like a man whose senses were focused on only one thing—getting these people to Palestine. Like so many Polish Jews, he had been a Zionist all his life; now he was the undisputed leader of the refugees. He must have been in his forties, but down in the cage, he looked ageless.

His lone voice, shouting out of the barbed wire, seemed even more terrible than the babel and howling had been. He was the voice of the *Runnymede Park*, the voice of trapped Jews living in a ship named after the site of the Magna Carta. He was the spirit of the new *Runnymede Park*, and each of us standing up on the bridge, looking into the cage, knew that he was the new Jew.

"What do you think of their taking you to Hamburg?" one of the correspondents shouted to him in German.

"They are new Hitlers. If they were not like Hitler, would they take us to Germany?"

His answer won the approval of the cage. The people shrieked and applauded. "Yes, yes, they are new Hitlers." They took courage from his courage. It was hard to remember that these were the same people I had seen coming off the *Exodus 1947* in Haifa. These were no longer the tired, bewildered, battered Jews mourning Bill Bernstein, Hirsch Yakubovich, and Mordecai Baumstein. Now they were defiant: trapped but defiant, defying England, defying the world.

While we watched, at the far end of the cage, high above the toilet, a mob of people unfurled a huge black banner supported on tall sticks. The Union Jack was painted in the top left corner and a purple swastika blazed inside a white circle in the lower right. The swastika was painted with gentian violet, the same gentian violet that covered their skin eruptions.

The applause which burst across the cage brought Colonel Gregson out of his cabin to see what was happening. He came to stand beside me while I took pictures of the flag and of the people grinning up at us, laughing at their huge joke.

The colonel grinned back. With just the right cynicism, he said, "They'll be pleased that you're taking a picture of the flag. They've been working on it for weeks now. They'll feel better now that they know someone's interested." He smiled some more as he looked around at his men who were watching the flag which linked these British troops with the Nazis. Then he left us to go back to his cabin.

Suddenly the bolted wire gate leading into the cage was unlocked and we were inside, swallowed up by the mob. A few exhausted bodies lay against the steel plates on the deck. We picked our way over them gingerly and then broke through the crowd to look at the two six-holer outhouses for 1,500 people.

The bodies, crushed up against us, were foul and hot. I knew I would never get the smell out of my nose and throat. Through the din, I heard people shouting, "Don't stand up here. This is good. There's air here. Come below. Come see our Auschwitz."

We followed the mob down a flight of slippery stairs without handrails. There on the floor of the hold was a charcoal drawing

The British have just announced they are taking the people on the ships to Germany. They select me to be the pool correspondent to represent the American press. Aboard the Runnymede Park, *I watch as the refugees raise a flag. They show their defiance of their British captors by emblazoning a swastika on the British Union Jack. The photo becomes* Life *magazine's Photo of the Week. The so-called hospital ship is a prison ship with an iron cage over the deck; next to the cage is a wooden latrine with six holes that is supposed to serve the 1,500 people aboard the ship. Below decks, the hold turns into a prison pen.*

The prison pen becomes their living room, their dining room, their bedroom, as they squeeze against one another. They have just learned they are being sent to Germany where, once again, they will be put in prison camps.

Inside the prison pen the only light comes through a small opening covered with iron grilles.

of the inferno. The hot sun filtered through the grillwork, throwing sharp lines of light and darkness across the refugees' faces and their hot, sweaty, half-naked bodies. Women were nursing their babies. Old women and men sat weeping unashamed, realizing what lay ahead.

There were no beds in the hold. Each man, woman, and child slept on a brown army blanket folded neatly on the slimy floor. The blanket was each person's living space, his dining room, his bedroom, and his study. Sometimes three or four people lay on a single blanket. Each man's space was bounded only by the dimensions of his body.

With a hospitality that had come out of a different world, a world that somehow had no reality here, a woman who looked as though she were in her late thirties invited me to sit on her blanket. She brushed it swiftly and handed her infant to me.

While I fondled the baby, she said, "My life is over." I asked her how old she was.

"Twenty-four."

"You mustn't say that; you mustn't talk that way. This will be over soon. You'll get there." I was saying all the stupid things one says in the presence of something tragic and enormous. But the woman was much wiser than I was.

In the hold of the Runnymede Park, *a twenty-four-year-old mother hands her baby to me. "I'm going to live," she tells me, "so that my child won't be killed in a gas chamber."*

"No, I know," she said. "I'm wrecked material. Even the long humanitarian fingers which stretch out from America and touch us can't save me. But I'm going to live for this baby. I'm going to stay alive so my child won't be burned in a gas chamber. I'm going to live so my child can grow up in decency, without being afraid. There are no frontiers to Jewish hope."

Now more women in the vast hold began to hold out their babies for me to see. I realized later that the babies had been

"Take pictures!" the people cry out. "Take pictures. Show our floating Auschwitz to the world." I take pictures blindly.

The French offer them hospitality. But they refuse to go down. "We will go down only in Palestine."

wonderfully quiet, that there were hundreds of them. I was aware that it was they who gave meaning to this whole exodus. It was for them that their parents had languished in DP camps, quit Europe, fled to Palestine, floated in this hellish heat, and were now being returned to Germany, perhaps to be beaten with truncheons and dragged down the gangways while the Germans stood by and smiled. It was here in this filthy hold that the smoke cleared and you realized what the *Exodus 1947* meant to the British, the French, and the Jews.

The French had emerged with their reputation for asylum more shining than ever. To the Jews, this was one more mile in the long passion of suffering. They had had their full quota of suffering, it was true. Now they would be carried north to

Germany. But though some might be killed, and some die, they knew that ultimately—maybe in a year, maybe in five or ten years—they would reach their goal. Nobody could stop them. It was the British who had suffered the most. The injury which the *Exodus* had done to Britain would never be effaced.

Britain, I thought, had been great because of a certain magnanimity and nobility of character that had always emerged in time of crisis. Her political leadership had gone hand in hand with a moral leadership. The *Exodus* showed how weakened Great Britain had become. This was not a single misguided act by unfortunate and unhappy civil servants in the field. This was part of a tragic pattern of corrosion and decline. Later, in London, I found many British officials filled with a sense of guilt and uneasiness about the

I realize it is the children who give meaning to this whole odyssey.

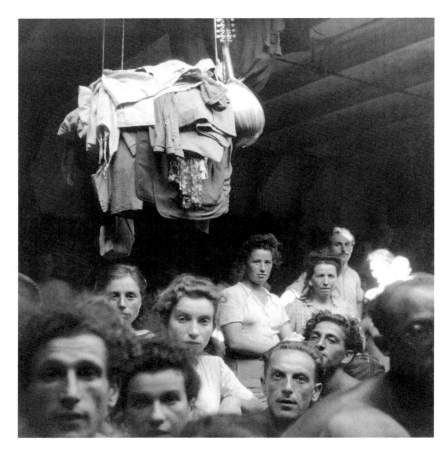

They hang the clothes they have salvaged and even a precious musical intrument in a swinging closet above their heads. They are people such as the world has never seen.

wisdom of forcing the *Exodus* refugees back to Germany. Liberals like John Strachey and Aneurin Bevan and P. J. Noel-Baker kept hoping to the last moment that something would happen, some new decision be taken, so that the socialist Labour government would not find itself in the role of sending back to Germany the victims of German fascism.

The women in the hold continued to lift up their babies and to beg me to take pictures of them. They would never see these pictures, but they were as proud of their babies as any more fortunate mother. Beyond the babies being lifted up, the people lay like the pictures that came out of the mass graves at Buchenwald on the day of liberation. Here was a head, here a pair of legs, here a pair of limp arms, and here an emaciated chest with the ribs

The hot sun, filtered through the grillwork, turns the prison pen into Dante's inferno.

The young people come on the deck to bid me farewell. As I watch the ships sail for Germany, a Haganah girl says prophetically, "Now you will see the birth of a Jewish state."

showing hideously through. I saw a few people sleeping, and wondered how anyone could sleep with all the noise that our visit created. A gentle, soft-spoken man explained it. "They can't sleep at night. It's too hot to sleep down here. So they fall asleep during the day, from exhaustion."

Hanging over us on rafters just below the iron grille was some clothing that a few fortunate ones had managed to wear on their backs in Haifa and had with them now in Port-de-Bouc. A raincoat hung over the bodies, and swayed as the ship swayed. A kind of square hammock, tied like a cotton bale, held underwear, jackets, skirts, trousers. There was a starched, immaculately preserved uniform. And, hanging like a body from a tree, there was a coat stuffed with clothing, filled out and swinging.

At Haifa there had been Mordecai Rosman standing with his arms outstretched, looking crucified in the bashed-in hull. Now, in Port-de-Bouc, there was a lynched and headless man swinging over the faces of tragedy and suffering and defiance.

I watched it all in silence, while a hundred people pulled at my notebook to write the names of their relatives in New York, in Chicago, in Haifa, and in Tel Aviv, begging me to send letters for them saying they were still alive. There were again a hundred questions I had planned to ask them. But now that I had the opportunity, I had no voice to speak, and all the questions seemed useless. These were people such as the world had never seen. The miracle to me was not that they had survived, but that they wanted to go on living. They wanted to go on living despite the betrayal, despite the power politics, despite the corruption and the double-talk. They wanted to go on living for their children, because "there was no frontier to Jewish hope."

Another woman came to hand me her baby. "Will it be cold on the way to Hamburg?" she asked. "We have no clothes and they have refused to give us back our baggage."

Mordecai Rosman came toward me. He saw me holding the baby, and his mouth twisted. "You are holding a fighter against the British Empire. These are the soldiers England fights." The tone of his voice, the contempt, made me shudder.

Disregarding Mordecai, only because this was their last chance, their last contact with the living world, the people pressed around me, bringing me more slips of paper with the names of their parents and relatives. Mordecai, looking like a half-naked Moses, screamed at the people.

"Why do you bother her with these petty personal problems? Why do you waste her time with your addresses? Let her write of our sufferings, our blood."

He turned to me, and I could almost hear an ancient prophet warning me, "Don't ask for our names."

A woman began to nod and weep softly. "We have no names, only numbers."

"Write," Mordecai shouted to me as though the woman didn't exist. The light fell in prison shadows across his bare chest. "Write that after the thirty-year-old Balfour Declaration, they have given us a new declaration; they have given out the Declaration of Port-de-Bouc. Write," he cried, with such fire and stabbing power that the sleeping people woke up and a few babies whimpered, "that the Declaration of Port-de-Bouc condemned forty-five hundred Jews saved from Hitler's Germany to a new life, a shameful life, back on the very soil where our people were murdered. We used to believe in the conscience of mankind.

"Write this, so that you may prevent this deed, so that our shame will not become real."

The people were still. Mordecai had shamed them into silence. They listened to him as once a people in that other exodus had listened in the desert.

"We still hope," he said, "that the world will not let us go to Germany, that the world will turn us back to our own land. Otherwise blood will flow in Hamburg. Otherwise the Nuremberg judges will be able to give a lesson to the German nation how once again Jewish blood can be shed without punishment.

"The English government has decided on the guillotine. For us it is no surprise. Those who sank the *Struma* and the *Patria* during the Nazi war would not hesitate now.

"We ask"—and his voice rang through the silenced hold—"where is the world of enlightenment? Where are democracy and humanity? Can the world be a silent spectator to this?

"The British hope to break illegal immigration. But we know our Jews. They will be afraid of nothing. Those who dared to revolt against Hitler and against the German war machine will not surrender even now."

He held my arm. "Give our greetings to all the suffering people in the world, in the DP camps, in Palestine, and in America. And give our heartfelt thanks to the French government and the French people."

He had finished. I could no longer bear to stand on the spot where he had talked. I began to move away, stepping over the bodies of the people.

Mr. Ashcroft came down to the hold to say that time was up. We started up the stairs. Mordecai shouted "Hatikvah." The people jumped up, their bodies squeezed against one another. They lifted the children in their arms to make room. The light fell in bars across their bodies as they sang. Their faces grew transparent with hope.

Men sobbed and continued to sing. Women lifted their heads, tearlessly crying. Ashcroft, bareheaded, stood at attention. His face twitched, as if he knew that they were reading the whole exodus into their song.

We climbed the stairs and once again the people began to stuff addresses into my hand. Inside the hot cage on the deck, a soldier jumped to open the gate and let us out. Ashcroft found himself held back by an old man, who cried, "I'm fifty-eight. I've lost twenty-eight people in my family. I lost my wife and my sons and my daughters in the crematoriums. I was in Auschwitz myself. What have I done? Am I a thief that you keep me in this cage under barbed wire? All I ask for is my piece of bread and a home."

The man's hysteria spread through the cage and others began to cry with him. There was no answer.

We descended into the launch and returned to shore. From the stone quay, we watched the ships. At exactly 6:00, the deadline hour, the *Runnymede Park* weighed anchor, blew its whistle, and slowly moved out to sea. Seven persons had disembarked, all of them ill. The ultimatum had been rejected. At 6:10, the *Ocean Vigour* followed, and at 6:15 the *Empire Rival* moved out into the Mediterranean, where an escort of three British warships was waiting. One of the Haganah girls near me, watching the ships set sail for Germany, said softly, "Now you will see the birth of a Jewish state."

Back on the wharf, the French residents of Port-de-Bouc set to work putting up carousels, sidewheels, and a large Ferris wheel for the carnival that was opening the next day. The little village was about to celebrate its liberation from the Nazis in 1944.

5

Hamburg

To the people huddled against one another in the cages, Germany, on the fateful seventh of September, seemed drowned in mist. From Port-de-Bouc, the three prison ships moved for seventeen days in a slow funeral march to Hamburg. For two and a half days, while they took on food and fuel at the Rock of Gibraltar, rumors spread through the holds that Bevin was relenting, that he was sending them to Palestine. But on the twenty-ninth of August, the ships untied the cords that held them to the mysterious promontory, with its miles of secret tunnels and gun galleries and its alerted troops. They were moving north to Hamburg.

Of all the weeks and months of their exodus, these days were the longest, the nights the most interminable. Nat Nadler, who had disembarked in Port-de-Bouc, described the food on the *Ocean Vigour*: "We got two meals a day. We would send a couple of men out of the prison cage for the food. For breakfast it was salty tea and a package of C-ration biscuits, an inch and a half by an inch and a half, ten in a package. When you broke them open to eat them, there were maggots in them. The evening meal was potato soup with the C-ration biscuits soaking in the soup, and for protein, the maggots were swimming around in it. When you're hungry, you eat it, maggots and all." The prisoners could talk of little else except the return to the death land. Each evening, in the Parliament of Peoples, they sang the words of the hora, their folk dance:

We have gone up to Eretz
We have gone up to Eretz
We have gone up to Israel.

They sang without irony. The waves of the North Sea beat an intermittent rhythm.

A thick fog hung over the Elbe River as the first ship, the *Ocean Vigour*, crawled through on Sunday afternoon, September 7. That night, thousands of DPs from the British camp at Bergen-Belsen gathered in "Freedom Square" carrying slogans:

EXODUS REFUGEES, WE COME TO YOU UNITED IN
THE STRUGGLE FOR FREE IMMIGRATION TO PALESTINE

THE EXODUS IN HAMBURG IS THE MARK OF CAIN
ON ENGLAND

There were Jews in the three prison ships who were graduates of Bergen-Belsen, of its German death camp and its British DP camp. They knew the mass graves well, the little hills of earth with wooden markers saying HERE LIE 1,000 DEAD . . . HERE LIE 5,000 DEAD . . . HERE LIE 10,000 DEAD. Twenty years later, I joined Elie Wiesel and Josef Rosensaft and other survivors of Bergen-Belsen to erect a simple granite pillar that had written on it in four languages: ISRAEL AND THE WORLD SHALL REMEMBER THE 30,000 JEWS EXTERMINATED IN THE CONCENTRATION CAMP OF BERGEN-BELSEN AT THE HANDS OF THE MURDEROUS NAZIS and the line imprinted on their brains,

EARTH, CONCEAL NOT THE BLOOD SHED ON THEE

At 6:00 A.M. on September 8, operations began. In the fog and drizzle, the *Ocean Vigour*, the "hospital ship," was tied to the quay at Hamburg. The *Empire Rival* passed Brunsbüttel at the mouth of the Kiel Canal on the way to Hamburg. The *Runnymede Park* was anchored off Cuxhafen.

Hamburg's wharf was lined with ambulance trucks, squads of doctors, and steel-helmeted British troops of the Sherwood Foresters, who had been stationed in Palestine the year before. There were also German guards. It was still dark. A loudspeaker from the dock told the refugees aboard the *Ocean Vigour* to come down peacefully. For a few hours it looked as though there might be no bloodshed in Germany. Women and children and families came down in a weary trickle. But by nine in the morning, the trickle ended. About half the ship refused to disembark in Hamburg.

Inside the holds, the people joined hands and danced the hora, singing passionately. Hundreds of troops were rushed aboard. The soldiers ran down the steps to the holds and with clubs and hoses forced the refugees against the walls. Bucket-brigade fashion, they passed the people up the slippery stairs, across the deck, and down the gangway to the wharf. Some were beaten with batons; others were kicked, pulled by the hair, and rolled down like felled trees.

On the quay, the British played popular American jazz to drown out the screaming. One of the refugees, dragged down the gangplank, shrieked through the music, "They shall not keep us from our homeland." Another one said simply, "We have returned. We have returned to Auschwitz and Bergen-Belsen."

The air had a familiar smell. A young man walked down slowly, his face streaming with blood. He tried to take his shirt off to show the correspondents his body, but five soldiers pounced on him and lugged him off to the train which waited alongside the pier. The refugees were loaded into old third-class wooden coaches which rumbled out of the harbor and through the German countryside to the village of Poppendorf, fifteen miles from Hamburg. Inside the railroad station, the Germans watched from behind barbed wire, while the Jews were herded into trucks and carried half a mile to the prison camp.

On Tuesday, the *Empire Rival* was tied to the dock at 6:00 A.M., and to the astonishment of the British, the people hurried down without resistance. Dov Miller of Brooklyn helped speed the people off. A little later, a homemade bomb was discovered inside the ship. The British detonated it in the center of Hamburg's deserted Barracks Square.

At 10:00, the *Runnymede Park* was lashed to the dock. For half an hour no refugee was to be seen on deck. At 10:30, a loudspeaker blared its order in Hebrew, Yiddish, French, and Hungarian, telling the refugees to land quietly or British troops would force them down. The refugees answered by singing in Hebrew, "Tekhezakna" (Be Strengthened).

The British carried down six stretcher cases. A few sick people, an old couple, and five children followed slowly. Behind them, the gangplank yawned emptily.

The British gave the people an hour and a half to obey the ultimatum. Three hundred troops, MPs, and Sherwood Foresters stood alert. They wore steel helmets, eye shields, and rubber arm guards and they carried teak truncheons.

At 12:15 the troops went aboard. At 12:45, five army firemen wedged powerful water hoses through the grille into the holds and drenched the refugees for a full minute. Shouts of defiance came from the holds. The voices of people singing floated down to the dock.

Ten minutes later, the hoses were turned on again, and the first resisters were hurried down the gangway. Pale-faced women with babies, children, and old men walked down, some staring at the troops with hatred, some averting their eyes as though the very sight of the troops was hateful.

Now the soldiers began to carry the fighters down. Six or eight soldiers carried each man and woman, holding their arms and legs spread-eagled. When the soldiers slipped, they dragged the people along the slippery gangway.

Sara Wiener, who had survived slave labor camps, death camps, and the death march, wrapped herself in a Zionist flag and looked at the German coast near Hamburg. "As I saw all the greenery," she wrote me later, "all the cleanliness and beauty, I cried for the first time during the whole voyage. I decided not to go down voluntarily, no matter what would happen. At the right time I lay down on the floor and didn't move. The soldiers ran down the stairs and started directing and pushing the people out. Those who resisted were taken by force, dragged, and some of them beaten. When they approached me I started to scream, 'I'm not going down. I do not want to step on German soil anymore.' The soldiers pulled me upstairs. I started walking between the two lines of soldiers, shouting and beating them. Nobody hit me back."

At 1:00, a murmur ran along the ship. Five British soldiers were tugging one refugee who resisted bitterly; his face was streaming with blood; blood and water covered his clothes and body. It was Mordecai Rosman. The British did not put him on the train, but turned him over to the MPs to be taken to a hospital with twenty-nine others.

The sound from the holds was an old familiar sound, the sound of heads being broken by wooden truncheons. Twenty-four refugees, seven of them women, were seriously wounded. Thirteen were sent to a hospital. Eleven were arrested as leaders.

The people were put on trains and taken to two German prison camps, Poppendorf and Am Stau, near Lübeck. That sight too was an old familiar sight—Jews standing in a cage while the Germans walked up and down smiling.

For a month, the British attempted to register the people, to get their names and send them back to the places from which they had started out on the long exodus. The people refused to give the British any information. They had only one answer, one word for all the questions.

"Where did you come from?"

"Palestine."

"What is your name?"

"Palestine."

"In what country are you a citizen?"

"Palestine."

The British became furious. "Not only will you not go to Palestine," they told the *Exodus* people, "but if you come on the quota list to go there legally, we will see to it that you go last."

The Jews had only one answer. "Palestine."

Epilogue

THE BRITISH MOVED THE people to winter camps, Emden, Wilhelmshaven, and Poppendorf. Here the refugees were permitted to live like all the DPs in the British zone. But they were taken off DP rations and put on the rations of the Germans, as further punishment.

The population in the two new camps apparently remained stable and the British thought the people were settling down for the winter in Germany. But the *Exodus* people were still on the march, and nothing could stop them.

They were led by the men and women of the Palmach and the Palyam who had traveled with them on the prison ships, posing as refugees. One dyed his hair red. Dov Miller of Brooklyn, pretending to be a cripple, wrapped himself with foul-smelling diapers, knowing the meticulous British officers would not go near him. Orphans, pretending to be sick, were helped into ambulances by their group leaders and smuggled out. Others escaped on trucks driven by disguised Haganah men. DPs from other camps nearby in Germany filtered into the camps that were holding the Jews of the *Exodus* and took their places. The British did not notice that their prisoners were escaping.

In little groups, they crawled out of the British prison camps and went down to secret ports in Italy and France, climbed on

Haganah ships, and traveled the whole underground sea journey, knowing that the way might lead to Cyprus, knowing that they might be killed like Bill Bernstein, Hirsch Yakubovich, and Mordecai Baumstein, knowing that the British might even send them back to Germany again, yet knowing that the British could not break them. Each *Exodus* refugee was given a special certificate by the Haganah, saying that he had been an *Exodus* refugee and was entitled to special privileges and a priority on the route.

Within a few months, the bulk of the *Exodus* people had left the British zone of occupation in Germany and successfully run the British blockade into Haifa. They were in Israel on May 15, 1948, when their nation was born.

They became her soldiers and workers and farmers. Some of their girls became officers in the Women's Army. Their boys went to the front. A young couple who had enlisted almost the moment they stepped onto the soil of Israel were dead. Mordecai Rosman became a high officer fighting in the battle of the Negev. The people of the *Exodus* had come home.

AFTERWORD

For many among the American crew, for the members of the Haganah, and for all of us involved, the voyage of the *Exodus 1947* changed our lives forever.

Models of the ship have been built, artifacts and plaques appear in the Smithsonian Institution in Washington, D.C., in the Clandestine Immigration and Naval Museum in Haifa, in the Mariners' Museum, Newport News, Virginia, and in the United States Merchant Marine Academy, Kings Point, New York.

We had hoped the *Exodus* herself would have become a museum, but unfortunately on August 26, 1952, she burned when a worker, trying to make her immortal, inadvertently torched her. She lies now on the bottom of Shemen Beach outside of Haifa.

ACKNOWLEDGMENTS

"Take pictures with your heart," Edward Steichen once told me. I think there was no other way to take pictures of these people, and no other way to tell their story.

For permission to reprint those portions of the story that first appeared in their pages, I thank the *New York Herald Tribune*, the *New York Post*, *The New Republic*, *Collier's*, and *Life* magazine. I also thank the publishers of the books *The Aftermath: Europe*, in the Time-Life World War II series, and the two-volume *Jewish Women in America: An Historical Encyclopedia*.

My thanks to Rabbi Marvin Hier and Richard Trank of the Simon Wiesenthal Center, for the creative use they made of many of these photos in their 1998 Oscar-winning documentary feature, *The Long Way Home*.

I am deeply grateful to Steven Spielberg and members of his Survivors of the Shoah Visual History Foundation, especially Michael Berenbaum, Michael Engel, and Daisy Miller in Los Angeles, for helping me find several people who were passengers on the *Exodus 1947*, whose stories I have added to this new edition.

It is hard to know how to tell Sharon Muller, photo archivist of the United States Holocaust Memorial Museum, Washington, D.C., and her associate, Lauren Apter, how much I appreciate their skill and weeks of work in arranging over a thousand of my negatives taken during this period in 1946 and 1947 and putting them in acid-free albums so that they may survive for another fifty years. The photos are now part of the permanent collection of the Holocaust Museum in Washington.

I wish to thank Bob Gilson, director of the School of the Arts of the 92nd St. Y in New York, for his masterful presentation of the photos held in an exhibition during the High Holidays. In a letter to me he wrote, "I hope I am not being presumptuous by urging you to be as generous as possible in sharing this work. Making your photographs readily available to museum collections (in particular) will help to insure that future generations will never forget the victims of the Holocaust."

The story was first bought by *The New Yorker* magazine in 1948 and edited by the incomparable William Shawn. But the owner of *The New Yorker*, Raoul Fleischmann, rejected it as being "too Jewish." Shawn telephoned Bruce Bliven, publisher of *The New Republic*, who bought it sight unseen and published it complete in three weekly editions.

I owe a deep debt of gratitude to Dr. David Altshuler, director of the Museum of Jewish Heritage: A Living Memorial to the Holocaust, in New York; Patti Kenner, a member of the museum's board of trustees; and Ann Oster, also a board member, for reprinting their own museum edition of the book as a salute to Israel's fiftieth anniversary in 1998. In their annual spring luncheon, they presented the book to five hundred women and men, many among them Holocaust survivors.

My special gratitude goes to Nancy Fisher, gallery educator at the New York Museum of Jewish Heritage, for her support of the photos and for her skill and tireless research in interviewing, not only my family and me, but several of the Oswego refugees for the Shoah Foundation—an oral history project that has led to a warm friendship.

I am profoundly grateful to my peers in the American Society of Journalists and Authors who awarded me their 1998 Lifetime Achievement Award as "a pioneering journalist and author whose books chronicle the most important events of the twentieth century."

My thanks go to many of the American crew who gave me of their time and memories, especially Bernard Marks, Cyril Weinstein, Nat Nadler, and Eli Kalm.

I am deeply grateful to the passengers on the *Exodus*, especially Uri Urmacher, Bracha Rachmilewitz, Sara Wiener and her husband, Chanina Kam, and Erika Klein, who told me how they reached the *Exodus* and what they did with the rest of their lives.

For his meticulous concern for my best interests, I thank my agent, Peter Sawyer, and his gentle boss, Fifi Oscard. For their help in editing, I thank Dan Levin and Helene B. Weintraub. For helping with the photo exhibits, I thank Joan Roth, Joan Schiff, and Charlotte London. For their tender care as they printed the negatives of my photographs, I want to thank Peter Goldberg and the late Sidney Stern. For framing the photos for the traveling exhibitions, I thank the Mark Gruber Gallery in New Paltz, New York. And for their ability to type as fast as I could dictate, I thank my three assistants: Diana Pollich, Aviva Goldish, and Idra Rosenberg.

At Times Books, I was embraced with more warmth and appreciation than I have received from any other publisher. First and foremost, I give heartfelt thanks to my editor, Philip Turner, whom I could phone day or night, who made the book his, who spent hours helping me select the hundred and one photos, and each time I recalled another incident, would say, "Put it in. It's great." No editor I have worked with has given me such empathy and understanding.

To others associated with Times Books I owe special thanks: to Heidi North, for her stirring jacket design; to Kyle Gallup for her original cover collage; to Diana Donovan, copy editor, and to Sybil Pincus, production editor, whose vigilance has been extraordinary; to Naomi Osnos, who oversaw the book's design with Helene Berinsky and who told me that she and Helene often had to put the photos down because they were crying; to Adriana Coada, for her artistry in printing the photographs and who told me that she, like Naomi and Helene, often had to stop reading because her eyes were clouded with tears; and to Lisa Schneider, Philip Turner's assistant, who helped me send out photocopies to people in the book, asking them to confirm my historical accuracy. I did this for their sake and mine, and for history, so that we may know that I have written the truth.

Index

Italicized page numbers refer to photographs.

Central Committee of Liberated
   Jews, 24
Children
   Bedouin, *33*
   on Cyprus, 107–8, *109*, 111,
      114–16, 117–18, *117–20*,
      121, 128–30
   DP attitudes toward having,
      114, *115*, 117
   in DP camps, *17*, *18*, 20–21,
      38, *42*, *43*
   education of, 121, 149–50, 151
   on *Exodus 1947*, *53*, 56, 58–59,
      60, *62*, 64, 65, 75, 76–77,
      78–79, *82*, 83, *84*, 86, 88–89
   in German refugee camps, 187
   and meaning of *Exodus 1947*
      affair, *173*
   on Port-de-Bouc prison ships,
      149–50, 151, 152, 169–70,
      170, 174
Churchill, Winston, 27
CID (British Criminal Investigation Department), 29, 48,
   61, 95
Cohen, Dr., 70, 90
Concentration camps
   DP camps as former, *14*
   See also specific camp
Crossman, Richard "Dick," 11,
   37
Crum, Bartley C., *10*, 11, 12, 16,
   20, 22, 26, 27, 34
Cyprus
   American crews as prisoners
      on, 93–94, 97, 107
   background about camps on,
      110
   bridge in Xylotimbu on, 119,
      119, 121, *122*, *123*
   British bar correspondents
      from prison camps in, 101,
      102

British decide against sending
   Exodus refugees to, 131, *137*
as British prison camp, 69, 84
British treatment of DPs on,
   129, 130
children await departure to
   Palestine from, 128–30
children on, 107–8, *109*, 111,
   114–16, 117–18, *117–20*,
   121, 128–30
conditions on, 93–94, 103–4,
   105, 107–9, *110*, *111*, 113,
   115, *116*, 118, *126*
creative life in camps on, 121,
   124, *125*, *127*
as death camps reborn, *103*,
   104, *116*, 121
as destination of *Exodus 1947*
   refugees, 49, 50, *55*, *56*, *58*,
   59–60, 63, 64, 65, 101
and dreams of Palestine, 94
education in camps on, 121,
   128
Gruber goes to, 101, *102*
Jewish transfers to Palestine
   from, 111, *112*, *113*, 125,
   128–30
"journalism" in, *126*
Mrs. Reid's interview of Bevin
   about DPs on, 123, 125, 127
smell of, 103–4, *105*
as threat to *Exodus 1947*
   refugees, 188
waits for *Exodus 1947* refugees
   arrival in, 101, *102*, 110,
   113, *117*, 123
water on, 93–94, *105*, *106*, 107,
   107, 108–9, *109*, *119*, *120*,
   121, *123*
Czechoslovakia, AACIP visits DP
   camps in, 11

About the Author

Born in Brooklyn in 1911, RUTH GRUBER earned her PhD from Cologne University at age twenty, then the youngest person ever awarded a doctorate. At twenty-three, she became the first journalist to report from the Soviet Arctic. That part of her life is recounted in *Ahead of Time: My Early Years as a Foreign Correspondent*. During this period, she also met with Virginia Woolf in London, who had been the subject of her PhD dissertation. The thesis was republished in 2005 as *Virginia Woolf: The Will to Create as a Woman*. In addition she is the author of *Haven: The Dramatic Story of 1000 WW II Refugees and How They Came to America*, which was also a CBS miniseries starring Natasha Richardson as Ruth Gruber; *Inside of Time: My Journey from Alaska to Israel*; *Raquela: A Woman of Israel*, winner of the National Jewish Book Award; and Witness.

Her photographs have appeared in more than twenty exhibits and documentaries, including the Academy Award–winning film *The Long Way Home*. In 1998 she received a lifetime achievement award from the American Society of Journalists and Authors. In October 2002, she helped dedicate Safe Haven, a museum in Oswego, New York, dedicated to preserving and learning from the experience of the thousand Holocaust survivors she helped shelter at Fort Ontario in 1944. Gruber lives in New York City and lectures frequently at venues around the country.